Coat On Coat Off Wet Feet

*To Geoff
with all my love
Linda
Christmas 2024*

Vicki Harrison

Coat On
Coat Off
Wet Feet

*How walking the South Downs gave me
inner strength for my recovery
and healing to help with my loss.*

Copyright © 2024 by Vicki Harrison
Published in the United Kingdom

All rights reserved. No part of this book may be reproduced or transmitted in any form or by any means, electronic or mechanical, including photocopying or recording without the permission of the author.

Paperback ISBN 9798327978898

Hardback **ISBN:** 9798327979161

www.coatoncoatoffwetfeet.uk

Cover design by Flintlock Covers

This book is dedicated

To my Partner, Michael, who somehow got me through my most challenging times of recovery and supported me throughout my new adventures and challenges

and

To my Dear Nan and Grandad, Jean and Dick Whittington who sadly passed in August 22 and April 24, who gave me the strength when I most needed it.

Contents

CONTENTS 17

THE YEARS BEFORE....................................11

9 MONTHS OF RECOVERY 21

FEBRUARY 22 – MY JOURNEY BEGAN 21

DECEMBER 22 & JANUARY 23................................35

GETTING BACK INTO NATURE WITH SMALLER WALKS 35

MY 14 MONTH ADVENTURE WALKS...................44

WALKING AROUND THE SOUTH DOWNS 44

FEBRUARY 23 – 'MY FIRST 10 MILER'....................45

WALKING INTO THE UNKNOWN 45

MARCH 23 – 'THE SKULL WALK' 53

THE CHARLTON GRAFFHAM & DUNCTON CIRCULAR – 20KM (12 MILES) 53

APRIL 23 – 'THE STILE WALK' 57

ARUNDEL TO AMBERLEY CIRCULAR – 25KM (15 MILES).57

MAY 23 – 'THE BADGER WALK' 63

EASEBOURNE & BENBOW POND CIRCULAR - 10KM (6 MILES) 63

MAY 23 – 'THE ANCIENT YEW TREE WALK' 68

WEST DEAN AND KINGLEY VALE CIRCULAR - 19KM (11 MILES) 68

MAY 23 - 'WALK OF THE HILLS'..........................73

BUTSER & OLD WINCHESTER HILL CIRCULAR - 30KM (18 MILES) 73

JUNE 23 – 'THE 100KM SERPENT TRAIL ADVENTURES BEGIN'... 82

PART 1 - MIDHURST TO PETWORTH 20KM (12 MILES) 82

'THE SERPENT TRAIL CONTINUES'. 88

PART 2 - PETWORTH TO MIDHURST - 23KM (14 MILES) ... 88

'THE SERPENT TRAIL CONTINUES AGAIN'. 94

PART 3 - MIDHURST TO PETERSFIELD - 16KM (10 MILES) 94

'THE SERPENT TRAIL FINALE' 100

PART 4 - HASLEMERE TO MIDHURST - 46KM (28 MILES) 100

JUNE 23 – 'THE MARINA WALK' 109

CHICHESTER MARINA AND DELL QUAY CIRCULAR - 18KM (11 MILES) 109

JULY 23 – 'THE WALK OF THE HARE' 113

SDW COCKING TO ARUNDEL 28KM (17 MILES) 113

JULY 23 – 'THE INQUISITIVE HORSE WALK' 118

WELLDIGGERS, HESWORTH & FITTLEWORTH CIRCULAR 9KM (5.5 MILES) 118

AUGUST 23 - 'THE WALK OF THE RINGS' 124

WASHINGTON, CISSBURY & CHANCTONBURY RING - 20KM (12 MILES) 124

SEPTEMBER 23 – 'MY FIRST ULTRA MARATHON FOR DEMENTIA UK' 127

Hove to Arundel - 42km (26 miles) 127

OCTOBER 23 – 'THE WALK FOR THE WAVES' ..139
Chichester to Selsey & Back - 42km (26 miles) 139

NOVEMBER 23 – 'MY COW SELFIE WALK' 148
Bepton, Midhurst Brickworks & West Lavington 14km (9 miles) 148

NOVEMBER 23 – 'WALKING 300 MILES FOR PROSTATE CANCER RESEARCH' 157

DECEMBER 23 - 'BACK TO CHILDHOOD MEMORIES WALK' 161
Petworth Park Circular 12km (7 miles) 161

BOXING DAY 23 TO 31ST MARCH 24 167
Start of the 800-mile Arctic Virtual Challenge 167

DECEMBER 23 – 'THE BUTTERFLY WALK' 168
The Durleighmarsh Circular throughout the year - 8km (5 miles)...168
Spring - March 23 169
Spring - April 23 170
Summer - June 23..171
Winter - Mid December 23 172
Winter - January 24 173

JANUARY 24 - 'THE MINIATURE SNAIL WALK!' 175
Bepton - Easebourne - Older Hill – Woolbeding Common - 22 km (14 miles) 175

JANUARY 24 - 'NEVER BELIEVE THE WEATHERMAN WALK'. **194**

LEVIN DOWN, COCKING, CHARLTON & WEST DEAN - 16KM (10 MILES) 194

FEBRUARY 24 – 'THE CHINOOK WALK' **202**

MIDHURST TO CHICHESTER CIRCULAR - 41KM (26 MILES) 202

MARCH 24 – 'CAUGHT BY THE DELIVERY DRIVER WALK' **208**

COCKING & BEPTON CIRCULAR - 14KM (9 MILES) 208

APRIL 24 - 'WALKING WITH MY HEART' **213**

MY 2ND ULTRA MARATHON – EASTER THAMES PATH FOR MACMILLAN CANCER - 50KM – (31 MILES) 213

MY FUTURE ADVENTURES & CHALLENGES **231**

MY RAYNAUD'S DIAGNOSIS AND JOURNEY .. **237**

DISCOVERY OF THE ULTRA CHALLENGE SERIES **250**

MY NEW PASSION 250

REFERENCES AND LINKS **252**

ACKNOWLEDGEMENTS **254**

ABOUT THE AUTHOR **256**

The Years Before

Rewind back to early July 2021 in fact 9th July, and I had been having problems for a while now, but carried on like you do, pretending to yourself that everything is fine.

The professionals remind you to keep an eye on any toilet changes, with those adverts on the television and the posters in the doctor's surgery constantly reminding you, but it is embarrassing thinking that you are one of those people who cannot do a number 2 properly. I simply thought, like others I am sure, *"It is just a phase I am going through. Sure, it will all be back to normal again tomorrow."*

Over the following weeks and months, I found that I could not eat as much, everything was upsetting my stomach. I could not go to the toilet properly, and everything down in that department was becoming an effort. Is it my age, 46? Are things simply just starting to go wrong? Is this what happens as you age?

Realising I just could not go on the way I was I knew I had to do something about it, but it is not the easiest thing to talk about. I tried to hide it and function as all was normal, but it was really starting to eat me up inside. I became more miserable, agitated, short temped and not the happiest person to be living with. God knows looking back how Michael, my partner, put up with me!

Panic mode set in as I did the thing you should never do when you are suffering with something – you start googling all your symptoms – it made things so much worse in my mind as there seemed to be so many possibilities about what it could be.

I remember making a call one afternoon to a friend, Emma, who I will be eternally grateful for, as the help she provided me that day is what devoted friends do. She had put something on Facebook about how she was suffering with Bowel Cancer (and only in her forty's too), and the post was about checking your poop and noticing any differences in your toilet habits. Wow, what timing that was.

Deep down I had been thinking for a while that I needed to do something about it, but honestly, I just did not want to deal with this. You hear all these stories of people having bowel cancer at an early age, and with my Mum being diagnosed earlier that year with Ovarian Cancer, and a couple of years before my beautiful cousin, Sharlene, passing away at only forty with Breast Cancer, I knew cancer was in the family.

Reminded by adverts that 1 in 2 will develop cancer, well the panic had really started to set in, that it was going to be me. Too many of my friends recently in their forty's were battling cancer, why would I be any different?

Phoning Emma whilst I was walking our dog, Samo, down the town, I knew she would be easy to talk to because of the way she has expressed so openly what was going on with her Bowel Cancer. I knew if anyone would understand it would be her.

When I spoke to Emma, she said *"Vicki, you need to phone the doctors now, this is not right. Your body is telling you something and you need to deal with this, you cannot go on, you do not want to be like me, and something be seriously wrong."*

After getting the guts to pick up the phone, I called the doctors later that day, knowing that Emma was going to check up on me to see if I had made that call. I had made an appointment and after seeing the doctor luckily for me, it was not Bowel Cancer.

However, it was not all good news, there was something, a reason these things were happening to me.

The doctor had said that I had a large rectocele (Pelvic Organ Prolapse). What is that I thought? I had never even heard of it, and I then spent the following days researching what it was, what it meant, what my options were, and what I could do to get my life back. I knew that I could not continue the way I was as it was only going to get worse without treatment.

In short, from my understanding, my pelvic floor had collapsed, and my poop was trying to come through the wrong hole. Something you do not want!! The wall had broken, and all that poop had built up inside of me, as it could not get out, to the point that I could not go. It needed a repair! It became so, so painful, to the point there were days I could not move and could not eat. The acid, the pain, I was doubling up in agony after food and remember it was trying to come out the top end too.

When I saw the doctor, still, I can remember her saying, *"Oh, we don't normally see that in patients your age. Patients are normally in their 70's. You should not be having that happening to you at your age. I will refer you straight away to the specialist as this cannot continue. But it is a difficult one and not as straight forward as we would like."*

Thinking here we go again, nothing in my life was every straightforward. If anything was wrong, it was never going to be a textbook case, I always managed to give someone that little bit of extra confusion or problems.

The doctor said *"I wonder which department you need? Do you need a gynecologist, or do you need colorectal? Because it is affecting both parts, your front, and your back? Let us try both!!"*

After a week, July 16th I had a letter come through from the Colorectal Department which I thought was fantastic. This is going to happen quickly now, but then after reading the letter properly I concluded that I had absolutely no idea of how long it would be.

Waiting and waiting as the symptoms were getting worse, I had no choice but to contact the doctors again. On the 2nd of August they had put me on stool softeners to try and help me go, so there was not that build up causing pressure and pain. In fact, stool softeners (something I always believed was simply for the older generation), became part of my daily ritual to try and help me go regularly, but they really were not helping, I think it had just gone too far.

As we approached October, I expressed to Michael I just could not go on like this anymore. I cannot move. I am in so much pain. I cannot toilet properly, its unbearable, in fact I am hating my life right now. The only way I could toilet was if I manually were to help myself to go, and this is wrong, I just cannot do it.

This was really, really getting me down and taking over my life. Nothing else mattered and becoming quite depressed, trying to continue as nothing was wrong, I found myself going into a deep black hole where there seemed to be no light at the end. There was nothing else the doctors could do either, I just had to go on that waiting list, and wait my turn.

Weeks on, and after getting frustrated that nothing was happening, I wanted to find out just how long it was going to take to speak to someone that could help me.

After phoning the NHS appointment line, they turned around and said, *"well, you will expect probably a phone call with someone about May next year."* This was 7 months away, and that was just for a simple phone call. Then it would take probably another 7 months to physically see someone and then maybe another 7 months before I could have an operation, which the doctor had already said at the initial appointment that surgery would be the only way to fix me.

COVID was also going through the hospitals, so I knew things were going to take much longer, as there were far more important cases that needing actioning. But for me, at this stage I just had to do something now. The thought of waiting for all those months, was terrifying me. What would I be like by then, when it had progressed so quickly from when I saw the doctor back in July?

Looking like my only option, after speaking to another friend, it was to make that phone call to go private. See a consultant, get an opinion, and see what needs doing and the costs involved. You do not know until you ask.

Here we go again, another phone call, and a nervous one too. If it is one thing I had learnt in the last few months, it was not to be afraid to speak to others about what is going on and getting you down, and defiantly not to bottle things up. It helped so much to talk to my friends as they all really wanted to help me, and I found out that often sharing your experiences can help others too. **Let us hope that that my journey and experiences can help others going through similar challenges too.**

This journey I was travelling on, was not one that I was just battling my health, I was battling with my mind too. I knew how expensive these things were; going privately for treatment is not cheap.

I had no private insurance, I had a little savings for a rainy day, but that was it. I had done a bit of research too and certainly could not justify paying that amount of money on myself, it was crazy, this should not be happening.

Remembering my dear friend Jess saying, *"if you were a car, you would fix it. You only need your car to go to school to do the school run and whizzing around, doing shopping. Vicki, you need to invest in your body now, you need your body. Your health is so, so important. You use it every minute of the day and without it you cannot function. You cannot look after your kids, you cannot do your work, you just cannot move on, so you need to get yourself sorted now."*

She was right. I think once she had said that it put it into a whole new perspective. Finally, I started to look at things so much differently. I knew I had to book myself into to a specialist to resolve my problems as I was damaged.

We often take so many things for granted; that you can eat, you can drink, you can walk, and you can toilet properly and I have realised that is not always the case. Your body is something you need to look after and listen too; something I never really did at this point; you just keep going on that daily life rollercoaster and continue with your normal tasks throughout the day.

Going back to the last call that I had made to the private specialist I made again when I was walking Samo! I made it when I was walking around the polo field waiting to pick Harry up from school. They said, *"Yes, Mrs. Harrison you can come up tomorrow evening at 7:30pm we'll see you then"*. Wow. I never expected it to be that quick.

From there on, things moved on quite quickly. The specialist I saw first, although he was not the correct one to fix me at that time, he recommended the lady who would be able to help me get my life back. I was happy that I had made that start to fix my broken body.

Although you would think that trip was a waste of my time as he could not help me, the visit was extremely helpful. After a lengthy conversation about various symptoms that I had shown through my child and adulthood years, he had suggested there was a clear indication that I could also be suffering with EDS (Ehler Danlos Syndrome).

That I should speak to my Rheumatologist for further investigation. Well, that was handy as I was seeing her shortly anyway about my Raynaud's treatment; something I had also suffered with for over 10 years, so it was the perfect opportunity to bring that up too.

It felt so good that I was not going mad. I had a probable reason as to why at my age, I was having these problems. It had made me feel better that there may be a reason for all that was going on with me.

The next appointment was to see the correct specialist at Frimley this time. She was lovely and said, *"Yes, we'll be able to operate and fix you up, not a problem, but we'll book you in for some further tests first to come up with a plan and see what we are actually dealing with."*

This was not just a regular rectocele either, it appeared as quite a large one and I needed it sorting soon too, because you know when you are getting older, things make their way south! Well, something I did not really want to be walking around with was my insides on my feet and that is all that was going to happen.

On the 18th of November, I went for a Colonography which was one of those most unpleasant experiences you could have, but I had no choice as they needed to see what the picture was before they could speak to me about my full options.

Sometimes you must just put your big girl pants on and deal with it. You find the strength from somewhere and to be honest you have no option if you want to get fixed. Later, I then had a CT scan on the 6th of December and the consultant said they were happy to operate, they could see the issues and what needed doing to fix me up and I had to wait now for a date to come through.

However, because of COVID they could not do anything yet. Unfortunately, it was affecting both private and NHS doctors as they could not book anyone in for operations unless it was for Cancer treatments or emergencies which I understood, but I just could not believe it. I was so close but so far.

Finally, I got a letter come through for February 28, 2022. That was my operation day. It was after that day that my world changed and although at the time, it was the hardest thing to recover from and I thought that things would never be the same again, it was the best thing I could have ever done for myself.

My New Journey was about to begin.

9 Months of Recovery

February 22 – My Journey Began

At first, I had to recover from my operation and although they try to prepare you for your recovery, providing advice and guidance, it is something you can never really prepare yourself for fully.

It was a major surgical operation, and it would be at least 12 weeks before I would be getting back to normal! Well for me, I almost knew that this was not going to be as straightforward as a normal recovery process would go, this is me we are talking about!

Especially as I had already had a funny turn when I asked the nurse to go to the toilet after my operation. I remember her saying" of *course, we will bring you a commode"* and I thought, I can do this no problems, I was flying high and feeling on top of the world because of the pain relief.

I sat on the commode and remembered saying to the nurses as they stood away by the doorway *"I'm going, I'm going!"* Well, they thought I was going for a pee, but I was actually going flat on the floor.

The next thing I remembered was twelve people standing over me shaking me and saying *"Vicki, Vicki, can you hear me, wake up, wake up"* I could hear them, but I could not respond. It was such a weird moment and a very scary one when coming back around, I really had frightened myself, and them.

Then to top it off, I remember before going in for my operation, that a lady had come around to ask what I fancied that evening for dinner. I thought why not go for the Salmon and Hollandaise sauce, it sounded fantastic especially topped off with a treacle sponge and I felt like I deserved a treat.

As it came in that evening, I tucked into my salmon, completing forgetting about the sauce and when I got to the pudding, I thought that looks nice rich custard. Well, you can guess what happened next.

Never put hollandaise sauce on your treacle sponge, it does not go!! But I was so desperate for that sponge and did not want to be rude, so I scraped it off and continued tucking in.

Well, I can still hear to this day, the laughter the lady had when heading back into the kitchen with her trolley. It could only be me to do something like that. What hope did I have now for a normal recovery, after doing such a stupid thing!! I had no chance really.

But set aside this, the hardest bit for me was not the actual recovery from the operation, even though that came with extreme pain, infections, packets of painkillers and antibiotics, it was how it messed with my mental state and how it took away my ability to walk properly.

Never was I prepared for the fact that it took me nine months to regain my walking capabilities, this was the EDS part kicking in now too. The frustration and the anger I had with myself in not being able to put two feet in front of each other and walk normally was truly overwhelming.

For the first week the surgeon told me to only be on my feet for five minutes, the second week it was ten and the third week was fifteen. This recovery journey seemed never ending and I was only three weeks in.

Overtime, I was able to be on my feet a little bit longer, but not do the normal things like lift the kettle, do the hoovering, don't bend down or do the washing, no shopping, all those things that you take for granted that you just get on and do. But I understood that its standard practice when you have had major surgery so had to just go with the flow and do what I was told.

Remembering when I first came home from my operation, the fear I had of those major stairs to conquer as we live in a first-floor property. I knew once going up those stairs, and once inside, I was not going to see or feel the outside for a while. It would only be through the windows which was tough because I loved being outside. I loved walking before I had my operation and feared the future. The doom and gloom were setting in.

Really missing getting outside, breathing in the fresh air, walking with the dog, all those things that you take for granted, I began to get fed up and feeling low. That feeling when you simply wake up, sit up, put one foot in front of the other and get on with your day, for now this was something I just could not do yet.

The first time I managed to get down the stairs to go out in the garden, was during late March 22 (a month later), and it was complete bliss. Tackling those stairs for the first time though was extremely painful. I was so determined to do it though, whatever the pain gave me, as I needed to feel the air again on my face as I was struggling being couped up indoors.

Finally, I did it, although it took me a long time to walk to the bottom of our garden, what normally would take me 1 or 2 minutes, would now take me 10 to 15, plus I felt like I had climbed Everest. But I did it! I was so pleased with myself.

Walking was not easy anymore. I had to squeeze my legs together, I would grip my pelvis in and hold my knees together to support everything in its place which would also help with the pain.

The pain was so hard to deal with and it was just like I had been hit extremely hard in the pelvis area with a cricket bat. At this point, I started to get terribly upset and scared that I thought I would never be able to walk properly ever again.

Those first few weeks of trying to walk again, my legs were like jelly. I would step outside, and you could see in my face that I was shaking, my legs were trembling, and they had no strength in them. They had become so weak, and I had forgotten how to walk.

I had become this person that just waddles along whilst trying to hold everything in and making sure that I did not have an accident as well. It was petrifying at times. I had to retrain myself how to walk and this is when I developed my 'Penguin Walk.'

With perseverance and listening to my body when it had had enough, which yes, I learned the hard way by pushing myself too much too soon, I started to get finally outside more regularly doing small waddles out to the garden, venturing out to the field behind us too.

When things got too much, I turned to my dear friend Amber who at the same time was recovering from Breast Cancer. Even though everything she personally was going through, she still found energy and time to help me through my recovery. Understanding that I was not alone, even at times when I felt it, she gave me the encouragement to keep fighting and not give up. We found that sharing our hardest and lowest times with each other, finding those positives in everyday meant we could move forward with our lives, pushing through our barriers and being there for each other.

Amber knew how hard it was for me at the moment too, as not only did I have all this 'learning to walk' problems to contend with, but my Mum was also recovering from her operation for Ovarian Cancer, my dear Nan had been diagnosed with Dementia, and I had so many different things to process.

My grandad, in his nineties, became nans carer during this time, which came with its own challenges and worries. I became extremely frustrated with myself yet again, as I could not do anything to help, other than be at the end of the phone. I regularly make daily phone calls to make sure both nan and grandad were ok, to which my grandad kept replying *"don't worry about us we are fine concentrate on getting yourself better."* I could always tell by the tone of his voice what type of day he was having; he would often tell me a porky.

After booking myself in for CT scans during April and May to check all had gone ok with my surgery because of the intense pain I was still having, I booked myself in to see Becky at Perfect Motion Physio for help in June when it simply became far too much to cope with.

Becky, a local specialist in Women's Health Physio, literally saved me. I broke down at my first appointment as someone was finally able to help me walk again, just how I did before. I was at the lowest I had ever been thinking my life was over and I thought I had done the wrong thing in having the surgery.

Although I was able to toilet and eat now, I still could not walk properly, but there was hope finally at the end of a very dark tunnel. She explained to me that I would get there but prepared for a long road ahead, up to a year of physio. I just couldn't believe what was happening.

Becky was so helpful in explaining what was going on with me. I had a 'Hypertonic Pelvis,' which in my understanding meant that my pelvic muscles had locked up so tightly, that they were like rocks in the inside of my pelvis, which in turn was stopping me from walking. It was on a rejection mission. The muscles were so tight and so painful that I needed physio to slowly release them. But due to the pain it was going to be small and often visits to work on those muscles both internally and externally.

The muscles had become so tight from the surgery itself, plus the infections afterwards, plus then throw trying to walk too, my pelvis was scared, and so was I. My pelvis did not want anything else happening to it. As I started walking and using my muscles, it was just having a hissy fit, going on strike and stopped me from walking.

At the same time, with all this walking trouble, I was also having real trouble with my waterworks, in fact every few minutes I was needing to go to the toilet. Something I did not realise when your Pelvic area malfunctions, your insides can too. I can remember counting those days I went over sixty times in a space of a day.

My life was being taken over with becoming absorbed by the bathroom and trying to walk. I still would have bowel issues too; I would block up so easily and I had to make huge adjustments to my lifestyle to help with my recovery.

Having to come off caffeine to help with my sensitive bladder, meant no coffee, no tea unless it was caffeine free, and it was something I was not prepared for or even aware that it would have such an effect. Then with the withdrawal of caffeine, came the headaches and then frustration crept in. This was so much harder than I had ever expected.

Overtime, although my body was finally getting healthier inside, this did not help my mind. It was a real, challenge, and yes, you expect things to be slower, and that you have got to slow down and allow your body to heal, but I truly just was not prepared for the not being able to walk part.

After four months of regular physio, although I still had lots of pain to deal with at the same time, I just kept pushing myself forward, as well as having the old meltdown and wanting to give up. I knew that I had to just carry on and continue to put one foot in front of the other and get back to a normal life. It was not going to win.

Persevering with my physio and my 'Penguin Walk' which I had been doing for seven months now, September 22 arrived. I started to do the school runs and a challenge that was. I can remember walking from the car park, which was only a little way to the school entrance, and it would take what seemed forever.

People looking strangely at me wondering what was going on and I am sure they thought I had an accident down below due to the way I was walking and gritting my teeth together.

I kept trying to be positive, taking each day as it came. Each time I went for a walk, it really did take out of me. I was exhausted and I really had to rest up in between. That went on for weeks and weeks, but I did get stronger and out for further walks.

Then in November and December, I managed to start walking further afield as I started to believe in myself and regained my confidence once again. However, it was still not proper walking, it was still my classic penguin walk. I was still trying to hold everything together, which in turn hurt my hips, my back, and my knees.

My feet became sore because I was not naturally walking, I was still so scared about what was going on with my body. So, it was a real, tough recovery and a fear of not being able to walk again was terrifying.

Think I had built myself up so much and I remember people saying to me, *"you're never going to get back to that mileage you used to walk for months yet, it's still such early days, you know."*

In my head I knew that, but I wanted to get to five miles by the end of December. They would all say," *it's too much, it's too soon you need to take it slowly."*

Personally, to get me through this, I had to set myself a goal because otherwise I was going to crumble. My mental state was crumbling already, so I zoned in, and I pushed myself mentally every single day. I took extra steps, and I kept going and going, pushing myself and putting one foot in front of the other.

To help with my recovery, alongside the physio, I started swimming again and tried Iyengar Yoga which really has helped so much in my recovery both mentally and physically. It has enabled me to learn to breathe properly again, which is something Becky mentioned in my initial assessment that I was not doing correctly.

Something I did not even think about as I thought there was only one way of breathing, you breathe and you are alive, you do not and you are well, not here, simple. But no, my lower part of my stomach was also holding on to the pain from my pelvis, and I was not using that part to breathe, so it was something else I had to work on too!

Having an amazing supportive Yoga Teacher too, Claire, she understood my journey and wanted to help so much, to help strengthen my body, my core, and my soul, which even today she provides that strength continually.

Throughout my recovery, and through my probable stubbornness but also determination, and inner strength, I fought my mind and my health back to fighting fit.

At times, I lived in fear of undoing all the surgery and the recovery I had made so far, but I had to persevere and mentally get over that fear block I had put inside my head.

It was not easy, and it was one of the hardest things I have had to ever go through, but I look back on it now and that was just part of the journey to get me where I am today. If I didn't have the operation, I really do not know what state I would be in today.

I pushed myself forward, I set myself a goal and I did not give up. I got through it with the support of so many people and will never forget them.

This is the reason now why I have the new love for walking, stronger that I ever did before. When something threatens you like that, and you think you are going to lose it, plus you have been working so hard to get it back, it becomes more meaningful, and you never want to be in a position where you would lose that again.

Pushing myself further and setting myself a new goal that on the first anniversary of my operation, I wanted to walk ten miles. I had a new purpose, a new goal.

I knew this would be tough, and people thought I was mad as it was still to early after my operation, but I was ready. This was going to be such an achievement not only to reach to the walking standard that I had before my operation but go over and do ten miles in one walk.

From that day I have found a new passion in walking, and I have taken myself to places that I never knew existed. I have found new confidence and strength in myself, and I have also become a challenger, challenging myself and taking on new challenges. I have learnt to appreciate and take care of what I have and remember how sometimes you must change your ways to improve yourself both mentally and physically.

Yes, it is tough, it is hard to change those ways that you have always done, those ways you are set in, but they are for the better. I look back now and yes, it was the best thing I did, but at the time I questioned whether it was the right or wrong thing. Doubting myself that I had made the wrong decision.

Here I am taking you on my journey over the last 14 months from when I did my first ten mile walk in February 23 to where I am today May 24 preparing for my 3rd Ultra Challenge.

Please note the km/mileage are approximate route lengths and are based on the routes that I took, including the wrong turns! I used a walking app, and this may slighter differ if you choose to take on these walks.

Over this time, I have enjoyed walking all over the South Downs area, places in Surrey and Hampshire, and I share these most favourable walks with you. I have also shared my experiences of my completed 2 Ultra Marathons and my 800-mile Arctic Challenge Training plan, walking you through the routes which have been extremely challenging but extremely rewarding.

I hope you enjoy my journey as much as I have.

December 22 & January 23

Getting back into nature with smaller walks

December 22 was one of the hardest times I found myself going through because not only was I dealing with my frustrations of my own personal recovery but due to other things going on in my life with my grandad, my stress bucket began to overload. I simply was not coping.

Grandads' hallucinations had got to the worst they could ever get. Followed by a scary and emotional event on New Years Eve, followed by other events taking me to A&E for a 12-hour visit, with a very confused and frail grandad. I just did not know what to do anymore and I normally found a plan for everything.

I had finally realised that I was not coping with what had been going on since Nan had passed in August 22. It hit me like a bus, and I fell to pieces. At this point, I had to step away and let other family members take over before it broke me completely, this was the hardest decision I had to make.

Choosing walking as my therapy, to process what was going on as I felt tremendous guilt that I was letting my grandad down, I got out in the fresh air to help me and started trying to walk more.

Deep down I knew I had to take a step back before it broke me completely and then I would not be able to provide the support that I did in the following weeks and months.

Luckily, living in the countryside with access to fields right on the back of my doorstep, I had such a wonderful opportunity to get out when I needed to, whatever the weather was doing. I would brave it and venture out for a 1 or 2-mile walk. Maybe sometimes longer depending on how strong I was feeling.

Often, deer hopped across the fields, or I stood watching the farmers plough ready for their crops. At times it was simply watching and listening to the birds of prey above, as they were scouring for the little field mice hiding in the grasses.

It was the perfect place to start my initial recovery walks as well as dealing mentally with what my mind was doing. My physio treatment had finished and feeling confident now to get out further than just walking around the block, I finally was relearning how to walk properly again.

Today as I started making my way around the edges of the fields, I could see all the white flowers popping up, the hedges were full of berries, and the birds were singing their happy bird songs. Something very uplifting about listening to the birds, certainly helped to lift my spirits.

I would head down the back of Midhurst Rother College, where often in the background you could hear the traffic whizzing by in the distance or the kids playing down in the school field. If you walked here during the Summer, you could often hear the echo of the ice cream van as it went down June Lane.

For now, it was Winter and this route when it had been raining, used to gush down the sides of the field with deep muddy water, making it very tricky to walk. At points along the route, it had made deep grooves in the ground, and I remember a time when Harry walked with me, where he could get in the grooves and hide as they were so deep.

Approaching the bottom of the field by the school, we would reach a sandy patch where Samo our dog, would always have a funny five minutes, suddenly switching to puppy mode, going mad when the sand hit his paws. For me though, walking on sand was always a bit more difficult but with perseverance I made my way through.

This is a lovely nice short hour route, which is just what I needed to start working on for my strength and recovery. I would walk through the wooded part at Whiphill and around the back of the fields, where I would then head back home. This route was enough to do daily for me to strengthen my legs and hips, and mentally prepare myself for longer adventures.

At times my mind would be in the right place, and I would venture for the longer version across the other fields and down to Woolbeding, but initially until I was truly confident in myself, I would start off doing this shorter route, which was reasonably flat with only a slight increase as you go up Whiphill.

The feeling of just being back in nature again, smelling the countryside air, listening to the birds, and appreciating what nature has given us, it was just bliss. I had almost forgotten just how I loved being outdoors. This really helped my mental state and gave me hope and strength once again that I was finally regaining control of my life.

Proving to myself that I was coping, and that I was pushing myself forwards, I continued doing these walks for my physical health and for my mental health too as these last few weeks have been so hard with my dear Grandad since we lost Nan.

Suffering with his continued bad hallucinations, and what we identified later as Charles Bonnett Syndrome, to do with the loss of his eyesight, he became very unstable and frustrated. His physical health was worrying and trying to get that help he needed became a battle too.

Walking really helped me, giving me thinking space and time to process everything that was going on. It allowed me time to think about how I could best help Grandad get through these tough times dealing with the loss of Nan. They were married just over 70 years before we lost her, so it is extremely hard for him, and seeing him trying to deal with this loss, pretending all is ok, when in fact his heart is so broken, was heartbreaking and so was not being able to help him. Walking was defiantly my therapy, to be able to simply be outside with no phone, no music, unless I felt the need to listen to relaxing tunes to help me unwind. Walking had really helped, and I could understand why people recommend getting out in the fresh air.

The next few weeks as I became stronger, I chose the longer route and my favourite time of the morning to walk was sunrise before everyone got up. It is always an incredible special time especially when you see that sunrise making its way over the fields, and then heading down to the riverside where you could see the sunlight coming through the trees and the reflections on the water.

Today it was frosty, and it was such a magical picture, where the spiders had been busy leaving their webs overnight. The sun was glistening, lighting them all up. I even remember taking a photo of this moment and sending off to Meridian Weather and it featured on one of their weather reports weeks later.

As the weeks went on, I chose to do the longer route more often. I would always look to see if I could see the wildlife here by the river, hoping that I would get that glimpse of the kingfisher on the edge of the bank. But I have never been that lucky yet, there is only one place that I had seen the kingfisher, and that was down by the Cowdray Ruins, a day which I will never forget. It is one of my all-time favourite birds and I was so lucky to get a photograph of it that day.

Recently where it had been raining so much the pathway around the river became challenging work to walk. It was very muddy in places, and you had to straddle to walk the pathway, or walk through huge wet areas, making your walking boots and socks saturated. Luckily now, they have put new decking down to extend the walkway, which is extremely helpful as the river does flood and at times it can make the area impassable.

You also were lucky on this route if you ventured down here when the wild garlic was out, normally around May time. There are patches where the wild garlic would take over, and it was a lovely smell as you walked through it, the aroma was amazing and reminded you of that tasty garlic bread or garlic butter.

Today I was also lucky to see a bird of prey sitting on one of the branches above, then it swooped down in front of me, obviously had seen something in one of the fields below. The trees were overhanging, so it hid quite safely away, watching until the time was right to make its move. I didn't manage to get a photograph of this one today, because it moved far too quickly, it always knows when you want to get the camera out.

It amazes me that so many trees have fallen over here too recently. They rest on other trees below, and even though they break in places, it is amazing to see that there is new life coming out of them. Sometimes it takes something bad to happen in life, and something to break in you, for you to branch off in a different direction and flourish like a tree branch. That is what I have done, something broke inside me, but after fixing me up, I have this new journey now and it is walking, and I love it.

I love being. out in the fresh air and there is something different about the way I walk now too. I take more notice of nature, wherever I walk. I am looking to see what snails are crawling up the leaves, what animals I can see or hear in the distance, hearing the rustling of the leaves as I see the squirrel shoot up through the branches and taking a leap of faith as it jumps to another tree.

You appreciate all the seasons and start to notice how things have changed. Caught up in the rat race before, having a busy home and work life, I never noticed what nature had to offer, but now things have changed.

Since having my operation, that is one thing that I have done. I have slowed down and realised that different things matter now. That is part of the ageing process too, you calm down, you slow down, and you appreciate what you've have, realising that things do not last forever. Every time I go out for a walk now, whatever the mileage, I come back feeling that I have accomplished something, and I have appreciated what nature has to offer.

Simple things are so pleasing, like when you hear and see the geese flying over. This is often their route, over the fields at the back of us, possibly where they head from Petworth Park in a straight line to Midhurst.

They always fly in formation too, in that V shape. It is always something that reminds me of growing up and living at home with my parents when the geese are out flying above, and the loud noises that they make, bringing back those cherished childhood memories.

As I walk around the riverway, the water's edge is hidden by high hedgerows, but in places you will see the water, and sometimes see the anglers sitting there trying to catch fish. There is something also relaxing about listening to the water, knowing you are in the country, but just having that water trickle by you.

With hardly anyone about, walking this route, it is just me and our dog Samo today, enjoying the tranquil setting. I can hear the buzzards swirling around at the top, hearing them over the fields, one, two this time. The little robin has also been showing its presence today and that is my Nan walking with me, which she has done since her passing.

This route I continued to do through December 22 and January 23, until I challenged myself to walking my first ever 10-mile route on the day of my first anniversary of my operation.

My 14 Month Adventure Walks

Walking around The South Downs

Sharing these walks with you, is a special moment for me. I have found some incredible routes here on our doorstep in the Heart of The Southdown's, and to be able to remember these with you, sharing my experiences of my adventures, I am hoping that one day, I can inspire you to, to go on your own discovery like I have.

Put your walking boots on and enjoy what nature has to offer us. I have selected my most memorable walks, month by month, sharing just what I experienced on the day of my walk, and I hope reading my adventures you will enjoy them as much as I enjoyed walking them.

February 23 – 'My First 10 Miler'

Walking into the Unknown

My first initial walk on February 28, 2023, gave me my *'Walking Addiction'*. I had prepared so much in my head the day before, where I was going to walk and how I was going to get through it.

Parking at the car park at the bottom of Cocking Hill, Samo jumped out the car excited ready for our new adventures today, something new for us both.

Not heading this way before, I had no idea what walking up Cocking Hill was going to be like. In fact, I didn't know that so many hills were waiting for me either and looking back now I am glad I didn't as it may have put me off.

Being in such a positive frame of mind, I was ready to do what I had set out to do, and it would take as long as it took. It was a beautiful sunny day, with a slight chill in the air, but perfect blue skies, with white cotton wool type clouds.

Walking up past the Cadence Cafe, which was not open at this point, as it was just after 8.15am, I made my way up over very flinty tracks to the top of the first hill. It was a tough hill to get up, which I think took about half an hour to climb. Once I reached the top, I stopped and had a breather and took in the views which were spectacular.

Suddenly, I had forgotten the pain of trying to get up this hill. It was not physical pain either, it was more just an out of breath pain, struggling because I was very unfit at this stage as I had not been doing the level of exercise that I needed to.

Carrying on, I could see all the sheep in the background as we approached the South Downs Way sign, showing that you could venture off the path in different directions. A huge, impressive boulder sat to the corner of the tracks to mark that point. I continued straight ahead up the slippery chalky and flint track going past the sheep in the fields dancing around either side of me.

Feeling so happy, I was smiling like a cheshire cat. This was my first real adventure out and meant something so much to me. I had my woolly hat on because it was still quite chilly, especially at the top of the hill, but soon I was feeling the warmth, and my coat was off. With my red, rosy cheeks, I was feeling so alive and proud of myself that I was doing this.

We continued through beautiful scenery of just fields and fields, and the views up here were breathtaking. It was so peaceful too, there was not anyone about this morning, just the sheep to keep you company.

Starting to get further along the hills, it was more of a grassy track than a flinty track now which I am so glad of because that flint was quite hard to walk on. Already I had stubbed my toes and you had to really watch where you were putting your feet, so you did not slip or catch your foot.

Continuing down the track we made our way through woodlands and came to the first junction point where I took a route right heading towards Treyford.

There was a beautiful memorial which stood at the top of the hill which said *"13 August 1940. Junker JU88A-1 crashed and exploded in Phillis Wood Treyford at 06:30 a.m. following an attack by No.43 and 601 Squadron Hurricanes during sortie to attack Farnborough. OBLT Oestermann killed. UFFZ Rossler, UFFZ. Seitz and Obergefr. Brieger bailed out and captured.*

There is a picture of this gentleman from the 13 August 1940 and there were various poppy wreaths laid around it. I stood there for a while absorbing where I was and what had happened, before starting a descent down through the tracks, passing back through some more fields, past a house, and then back up and round yet more hills. It was certainly a day for walking hills.

As we approached the next hill, I could see in the distance hand gliders were flying above. The sound as they would swoop around down in front of you, was spectacular. Not anything that I was expecting that is for sure and made that a memorable moment whilst climbing to the top of the hills.

Looking at my Alltrails App to see the mileage that I had done, I was about to approach the 4.5-mile marker. Crossing over the cattle grid down to a further hill, which looked the steepest I had seen yet, I knew I would need to climb it to reach my 5-mile turning point. It was the start of Harting Hill, and I felt like I was climbing up on my hands and knees at times but being so determined to make it to the top, I continued, whilst watching Samo just fly up the hill making it look super easy. What I would do to have four legs right now.

Approaching the top, I could see kites flying around us once again and it was certainly a place to see them all up here, I had already seen so many on my route so far.

Walking over to the peak of West Harting Down, I saw a beautiful stone monument called a Trig Point, which I had not seen before, but understand you can discover others along the South Downs Way.

It said *"The Harting Down was given to the National Trust in memory of Nicholas Bothwell, aged twenty-five, who died tragically on the 5 May 1987. A beloved son"*

Also, a compass of North, East, South, and West showing you how far various places where away, such as Farnham 18 miles, Petworth House 10.5 miles, and the Goodwood Trundle was just 7 miles away.

Reaching the 5-mile mark, which in a way I was extremely pleased about, because if I needed to continue then I had another few hills to combat. I sat with Samo for a good 10 to 15 minutes, just absorbing what we had done and how far we had walked.

The views from here were something I had never experienced before and did not realise just how far in the distance you could see. I really could not believe how far I had walked and all I needed to do now was simply turn around and head back home, but for now I took in the views, capturing every moment whilst I could.

Samo looked at me thinking *'I'm loving this too mum and think this is probably the longest walk I have done, can I do more now!'* What had I started!! He looked up to me with his gazing eyes and his funny smile as if to say, *"right mum, we have had our rest, are we ready to get walking again now please?"*

Off we went heading back to see the hand gliders in the distance, following the same route just seeing things differently. I noticed the Devils Jumps this time, which are a group of five large bell barrows and listed as a Scheduled Ancient Monument I later discovered.

Walking down the flint path, my legs were starting to struggle, and I really did hit my big toe a cropper, thinking I had done damage to it. I assume I simply was not picking my feet up high enough to get them over the big flint stones due to them being so weak now and tired.

Ready for a black toenail when I got home, I gritted my teeth, just putting one foot in front of the other heading towards the Warren Bottom turning and stopping at Cadence Cafe for a very well-earned coffee and a flapjack.

What an achievement, I am so pleased of my adventure today. That was my first 10-mile route and from that day, I just continued getting stronger and stronger. The experience was so exhilarating and rewarding that I decided that Tuesdays was going to become my walking day. The day for me to switch off, cope with the week that had just passed and prepare for my week that was approaching.

After walking for a couple of weeks I was loving this so much, that I wanted to have a real purpose for my walking, so I decided to raise money for Dementia UK after losing my nan only six months ago.

Starting to look online at charity walks which were happening this year, I discovered The Ultra Challenge Series, where I could choose my charity to raise money for, and there was one in September 23. This would be doable I thought, as I still had 6 months to train, it was based in Hove, walking the South Coast to Arundel and I wouldn't have to worry about travelling too far either.

Well, next thing I knew, I had pressed that button and decided to go ahead and do the craziest thing I had ever done. I had booked up my first ever Ultra Marathon (over twenty-six miles). I think when I told Michael what I had done, he thought I had finally lost the plot.

"You have only just started walking properly, and now you have decided to walk an Ultra Marathon, not even just a normal marathon, but an Ultra one, your absolutely nuts but just go for it if that's what you want to do." I think deep down, he knew that I am not one for giving up, however hard it may be.

Thinking of my crazy plans I had made, I then decided to contact a dear friend Claire, whom I have not seen since back in school days over 30 years ago. Seeing that she was posting her beautiful walks on Facebook too, I thought I wonder if she would like to team up with me and we could discover new routes together.

Claire was also going through tough times with her Mum and her recent Dementia diagnosis, and I thought walking would also be a way of helping her with her mum, as in my journey so far, I had really discovered that talking had helped me so much too. If I could help her in any way through the experiences I had with Dementia and my nan, then that would also be a positive outcome.

I asked her if she fancied joining me on an adventure - and it was just like we had never been away from each other. Stepping back right into being teenagers again, only 30 years on, venturing into unfamiliar places with our first being in March 23.

March 23 – 'The Skull Walk'

The Charlton Graffham & Duncton Circular – 20km (12 miles)

During early March, I decided to get a bit more adventurous and go for something a little bit longer, 20km and approximately 6 hours walking. Well Claire was certainly brave letting me choose the route today, knowing what crazy plans I was coming up with lately.

Starting at Charlton we walked up onto the top of Heyshott Hill, back over towards Graffham, Seaford College, over to The Cricketers, and from the bottom of Duncton Hill, walking back up the hill heading around in a circular route to where you first started. How hard could this be!!

Well, this was a completely different walk to what I had been doing so far. It had been raining, the fields were soaking wet, and we went through woods where it was extremely boggy. Remembering we were having so many laughs and giggles along the way, both thinking, who is going to go down in the mud first?

Catkins were out dangling from the trees, and glowing in a bright green, glistening in the sun. The bluebells had not come out, but you could see where they were going to be coming up very soon. We always said, we need to remember where these beautiful places are, so we can come back and see them in full bloom.

Following the Alltrails Walking App, which had been fantastic for me so far for planning new routes, we walked into Graffham, a familiar place to us both. Stopping for that essential coffee and rocky road at the Village Shop, we sat to refresh and enjoy the comfortable seats.

Heading back out, we continued walking through fields to the entrance of Seaford College and these tracks in places where ankle deep in water, our feet where soaked. At this stage we never knew waterproof socks existed.

Venturing through another waterlogged field trying to dodge the large boggy parts, we crossed over to The Cricketers Pub, where we made that particularly important stop for the essential wee and refreshing can of coke as by this time, we were both feeling the heat.

Discovering a beautiful little river over a quaint pretty bridge, we made our way behind The Cricketers, and then through a field full of sheep which was a delightful surprise.

Claire remembered at the bottom of Duncton Hill, there was an Ancient Churchyard, of St Mary's, which being an old church from 1795, had become derelict and overgrown. We had a quick peep in, but it was so full of shoulder high hedgerows and brambles, the headstones so worn you could not really see the writing on them.

Carrying on walking to the top of Duncton Hill we were both struggling to find the energy to take us back up, questioning the route I had chosen for one of our first outings.

But laughing and joking all the way up, about how far we had walked, how mad we were and when planning the next route to look at the hills, it had managed to help us continue up the grueling hill with a sheer drop the other side.

Taking lots of photos to remember our journey, they became remarkably similar of fungi and mushrooms that were growing all around. When we finally reached the top, the views took your breath away and you soon forgot how hard it was to walk to that point.

The warmth of the sun was now making it harder to walk and we looked forward to Charlton Woods which was approaching soon to take cover. Looking up at a tree as we ventured deeper into the woods Claire spotted a skull hung on a tree, which she was forever seeing on her own walks, something new for me.

Before we knew it, we were heading back where we had started. As I got in the car to drive away, I looked down at my hands and they had swelled up so much, and difficult to bend, something I had not experienced before.

By the time I had got home both my feet and legs really did ache and I think we both had blisters. I started to realise that I needed to invest in my footwear to prevent any future blisters and sore points.

Such an enjoyable walk and having someone else by my side when you are walking into unknown places, at distances you have not ventured on before, gave me comfort and safety.

The walk was so uplifting, and I cannot wait to do it again, so I have added it to my list, but next time I will even do it in reverse too!

April 23 – 'The Stile Walk'

Arundel to Amberley Circular – 25km (15 miles)

Fancying a more challenge route than our last adventure and with Claire being so trusting of me, I suggested to go for a circular route starting at Arundel, heading towards Burpham, through to Amberley venturing into North & South Stoke, through to Offham before finishing back at Arundel.

Being a bright blue sunny day, it was the perfect day to start on our adventures. This was the first time we had attempted doing just under 25 km walking, so we were feeling adventurous and nervous about whether we would make it back to the car.

Alltrails App told us it would take us just over 5 hours of walking, so it was defiantly quite a walk we were going to embark on, but we had both dogs with us for support, and we had taken plenty of water with planned stops on the way.

Starting our adventures, after popping in first for a takeaway coffee and humongous piece of shortbread from the lovely café on the corner, we headed off walking around the river Arun, which was such a tranquil and pretty place to be.

Being one of the first walks that I had been around the waterside, I found it extremely uplifting and very refreshing. The sound of the water is so calming, and it was something so different from my normal routes I had been discovering through the woods weeks before.

Beautiful, elegant swans swum along the side of the river which you could just see through the reeds alongside the walkway and looking over in the distance you could hear and see the train in the background zooming along. This route soon became named the 'Stile Walk,' as there were so many stiles to cross with a couple not being very sturdy and complicated.

From a distance you could see Arundel Castle which reminded me the time I abseiled down the tower for Chestnut Tree House in Memory of my dear friend Ambers Stepdad, who was a great supporter of the charity. What a fantastic experience that was, apart from climbing up over one hundred steps to get you to the top, and as you hung over the edge your stomach fell to the bottom first!

Approaching another one of those stiles, this one was an overly complicated, rickety old stile, which honestly, I do not know how it did not fall to bits in our hands when we were crossing it. There just seemed so many already and I think we counted over twelve in total on this route!

Walking conditions underfoot were dry at this point, which was lovely, the weather finally had been kind to us. Continuing walking through the pretty villages, we funnily enough bumped into Amber's mum, explaining that we were on our first major adventure in preparation of my Ultra Marathon in September. I think she must have thought we were both mad with our route as it was getting hot, and we still had a long way to go.

Progressing up a long and winding hill we came across the farmland at the top. We were so exhausted by this hill as this was only the second walk that we tackled serious hills, and still recovering from the first to be honest, so it certainly gave us a workout and we got very out of breath.

We stopped at times up that hill, but we giggled on the way and when we go to the top the views where truly spectacular and we soon managed to forget how hard it was on our hips and legs, as well as those blisters that were starting to appear. We had no choice but to continue and knew we would be paying the price in venturing out so far in the upcoming days, but as they say, "no pain no gain"!

A highlight for me was coming across the Belted Galloways enroute, always one of my favourite sightings as well as seeing an abundance of sheep over the acres of farmland.

Such a beautiful part of the South Downs Way that we tackled and to appreciate the views when we got to the top of the hill, was breathtaking. You could see right down to the river as it winded round like a snake, and certainly made you realise why you wanted to walk to the top. As we ventured back down the hill, we walked past Amberley Museum, and you could see where they had filmed James Bond years ago.

On our way back we spotted butterflies again, as well as colourful primroses around the sides of the route. We approached Amberley and thought it would be a perfect time to stop for refreshments at the Riverside Café, resting our very heavy legs and recharging with lunch.

Sharing a sandwich because we did not feel hungry at the time, we knew we had to recharge, and replenish our systems to get back to the start. The dogs laid down on the decking and just chilled out, as they were a bit shocked of walking as far as well!

Coming out of Amberley, we crossed over the road and made our way further around the river heading back towards Arundel. We discovered that mud still existed in places and this place was extremely muddy. Luckily, we did not have too many miles to go as we did get extremely wet feet plodding our way through the mud.

How I did not face plant myself in the mud I do not know. Pure luck, I guess. We were giggling about which one of us was going to go down first and if anything, it would have been me. But we managed to both stay on two feet and we continued over quite an impressive bridge, which then took us onto North and South Stoke.

We came across a beautiful little quaint church which was a lovely discovery. Theres something special about seeing these beautiful village churches. On the final part of our walk, we ended up walking back into Arundel, stopping at the Black Rabbit for a well-deserved refreshing glass of ice cool coke.

There was a huge seagull perched on the big red telephone box, watching to see who was eating so it could steal something off their plate.

Once we had recuperated a bit as not wanting to sit too long, in fear we would never put another foot in front of each other, we found that last bit of energy to get us back to the start line. We carried back towards the Arundel Wildfowl Trust and walked around the water's edge back till we got back to the car park where we had first started.

We had such a fantastic time and were absolutely beaming with achievement as it was just under 25km and took just over 5 hours, but worth every minute. It was refreshing, uplifting and we both were on such a high as we did not every think, we would be able to achieve such a lengthy walk.

We have never talked so much, which helped us get up the hills, to be honest. I remember having jaw ache that evening, as I do not think I have ever talked for so long! My jaw part dislocated having dinner, which I realised after my research into Ehler Danlos Syndrome (EDS) was quite common and something I knew I had to now look out for. I made sure on future walks I did not do so much talking but listened!!

Although this is a walk which I have not done since April 23, I hope to be doing it this year once again. I highly recommend it if you are ever this way to soak up the views of Arundel and the surrounding areas.

May 23 – 'The Badger Walk'

Easebourne & Benbow Pond Circular - 10km (6 miles)

During May 23, I started discovering a number of different routes around the South Downs that I could walk from home. Although it is hard to pick my favourite ones as all of them have had their unique views and parts to it, this one is one of my continued walks I still do today. It is a shorter 10km route taking me around 2 hours to complete and I always take my beloved dog Samo with me for company.

Choosing a circular route where I would head from home down through Cowdray Ruins, towards Easebourne and Lime Tree Walk. You would then venture on the footpath though the Cowdray Golf Course, which I was always a bit apprehensive about at first, as knowing my luck I would be hit on the head by a flying golf ball! But if you rang the bell before you set across the course you knew people would know you were there.

Feeling a bit out of place walking across the course, I triple checked my App and I was heading the right way.

Once you made your way through the course and out onto the other side you headed through beautiful sprays of Bluebells, it looked so magical and refreshing, a carpet of flowers and trees which then led you down to the John Cowdray Arboretum (3rd Viscount Cowdray 1910 - 95) which was established in 2000 and opened to the public in 2009.

Set in the vicinity of beautiful Cherry Blossom Trees not yet out in bloom, but you knew when they blossomed, they would be spectacular to see and such a fragrant smell. In one of the trees, I saw one of those Geocache boxes, but left it alone for others to discover.

However, we took a left before heading down to the Arboretum, through a gate and walking over to see the Famous Queen Elizabeth Oak. When venturing closer we reached an extremely boggy wet bit, which in places felt like you were getting stuck in the mud. Worth the trek over though as it really is such a special tree to see, fenced off to protect it.

Seeing Benbow Pond in the distance which is always a tranquil and calming place to be, I headed over to the bench for a 10-minute breather so I could enjoy that moment and watch the black swans on the water.

Alongside walking, you really do have to stop and sit to take in the atmosphere and beautiful scenery. Listening to all the birds chirping away, such a pleasant sound, and I often wonder about what they are talking about.

Continuing back on the route I walked up through the back of the fields which then took you on a smaller quiet enclosed footpath and a track up towards the top of a hill. You could see where all the badgers had been digging out dens in the sides of the banks and I started naming this one as 'The Badger Walk,' even though I never seen one, I knew that they were there.

On this day in May, the sun was beaming, the bees were enjoying the flowers, and the gnats were enjoying me! The bluebells in places up the track were just starting to slowly die off. The fields were full of green corn and the sun was shining and starting to dry everything out. It was a beautiful day to be walking, not too hot and with a gentle breeze.

Wandering up the track, you could tell that this was a route that the horses regularly go up, because of the deposits they left on their way. The large tree roots in the banks often had me questioning 'how did they manage to stay there without falling over'?

Once you had walked to the top, the beautiful views over the fields and the downs in the distance were spectacular. You would walk past a special monument called "Nathans Post" where it had written" He *does not die who can bequeath. Some influence on the land he knows."* Carved out of wood with a guitar at the top, a large acorn sat on a stand with a fox climbing up. Such a unique and cleverly carved monument to see with the downs behind it.

Rapeseed was in full bloom, and when we got to the top you could see these stunning two horses which came over to greet us. There were a few of them in the field as we got further along the track and I discovered three little beehives, which was something you started to see increasingly in people's fields.

Heading back down through Easebourne Street I stopped off at Cowdray for my regular flapjack and coffee stop, convincing myself that this was the healthier option, it did contain oats!! I sat on the bench enjoying the surroundings and looking down at my muddy boots thinking they will need a good wash along with my four-legged friend when I got home.

My coat had constantly been coming on and off during this walk as when you got to the top, the cold breeze hit you, but walking up the enclosed tracks to the top of the hill, it was a different story. Nice red, rosy cheeks!!

That is a walk that I have continued to do on many occasions. I have even started walking the same walk but in reverse as it can be a completely different experience as you see things you did not see first time.

Walking down these hills, instead of up is often harder than you may think, especially when you must watch your footings because of the looser rocks and muddy paths. Me being me, I was always going to find the wrong place to put my foot too but so far, I have managed to stay on two feet, but only just!

Certainly, something I highly recommend that if you've done a walk one way and you've loved it, do it again, but walk the other way around. Often the views that you see from the other way, can be completely different, and it's always worth on any walk discovering what nature has to offer from as many different aspects as possible.

May 23 – 'The Ancient Yew Tree Walk'

West Dean and Kingley Vale Circular - 19km (11 miles)

Another beautiful day in May and I had been very lucky with the weather so far on my chosen days to walk. Today I parked at West Dean Gardens and decided to go for a route which took me to Kingley Vale, which is a place that I had only visited once before, and a magical place with the ancient, enchanted trees as I remember.

Taking Samo with me today, we started our route walking through the old railway bridge first, which took us up to a steepish hill which when reaching the top was like a perfect painted picture, it was beautiful.

Luscious green fields, green trees, blue skies perfect cottonwool clouds in the sky above. We walked through these beautiful green trees and plenty of wild garlic shone with its bright white flowers on either side of the track. The aroma was amazing.

Walking past the shortened remains of a tree trunk, the moss had taken over it with ivy too, and it was like a smooth carpet covering by nature. On the side of it was fungi placed so perfectly, the way it was climbing up the side of the trunk.

From here it was an abundance of fields, everywhere you looked you could just literally see for miles in the distance, field after field. This was true beautiful countryside views; we are so lucky to have such views around us.

Walking up a flinty track, I could hear engines and people talking, and I realised that one of the tractors had got stuck in the field and another tractor was pulling it out; things were not really going their way at all.

Continuing further up the track we came to a crossroads which took us to either Chichester, West Dean or Chilgrove. I had an idea where I was, as I had previously done a circular route from Cocking through to West Dean and Chilgrove.

I ventured out on to the main road, continuing, turning right opposite the Pub, going up another hill taking us towards Kingley Vale. At this point, the sun was really beaming. It seemed to have only taken me just over an hour to get to this point, so I was making quite timely progress.

We started to make our way up through the trees and I remember getting to the top and it just being full of bright yellow heathers and gorse that you get in the woodlands. It was stunning, the vibrancy of this yellow-coloured bushes, everywhere you looked, and it made you smile like the sunshine.

Finally making our way into Kingley Vale Nature Reserve, which lies within the South Down National Park, we discovered the sign which told us that it covers 160 hectares of chalk, grassland, scrub, and woodland. I never realised it was so big.

Luckily, we had reached a nice bit of shade as we walked through the trees, because at this point, the sun was really beaming down and becoming very intense. I needed cooling down before walking back out onto the top again to more open farmland and woodland with no covering from the sun.

Making our way through the ancient yew tree forest we reached a bench where I sat down and literally admired the view. I had taken a flask with me and enjoyed a cup of refreshing tea, and an apple to boost my system with a bit of natural sugar. It was so perfect sitting there and absorbing the surroundings, not another soul in sight.

We had only seen a couple of walkers throughout the whole time we had been walking so it was an extremely peaceful place to be. Starting to head our way back down on a flinty path we then turned back down to the woodlands, which then took us again onto the public footpath. It was pure, just blue skies again, cloudy fluffballs and just luscious green fields and trees everywhere you looked. You could see more rapeseed in the fields, and it was the perfect summers day.

Approaching Binderton I had an idea of where we were, trekking across a lot of fields that had lush green grass, and the sheep had come up to the fence line to say hello. Continuing back on to some of the Centurion Way route it took us by the water's edge. We crossed over a bridge and walked besides a truly clear spring water river, which you can often see from the roadway. I then headed back over some hills, which were the hills that you could do on another walk I had seen on my app, it was 'The Hills of Goodwood' route, and one certainly for another day.

Struggling with my feet at this point, as they were extremely hot and sweaty, they were becoming uncomfortable as I could feel them swelling. By this time, I had learnt that you need to size up on your trainers because your feet do swell quite a bit. The views, you could see when on top of those hills were breathtaking, you could see the whole of Chichester in the distance including the Cathedral Spire.

Making our way up to The T Box, a horsebox café which I had remembered from a previous car trip I enjoyed a lovely slice of rocky road and a delicious cup of coffee, something that was becoming a bit of a ritual now when stopping!

I sat on the side of the step taking in what I had achieved so far. After a 10-minute stop, as I never liked to stop too long as I think I would find it hard to get going again, I headed down the main road now, as I think I had missed one of the turnings on this point. Something I had not yet done on my App, as they were always so precise in their directions and told you when you were off course, but today, I had misjudged the route and made my own path. Safely getting back down to the bottom of Goodwood Hill by the Weald and Downland Museum, I then took a left back down the pathway from Singleton and made our way down to West Dean where we parked the car.

Coming home I put my feet straight into a foot spa as they were quite sore and swollen at this point. I had done a total of 19 km in 4 hours, and although a few hard inclines, it was a brilliant route, and a very magical place as you get through to Kingley Vale, seeing the wonders of the Ancient Trees. A highly recommended route when you are venturing out that way.

May 23 - 'Walk of the Hills'

Butser & Old Winchester Hill Circular - 30km (18 miles)

Starting at the bottom of Queen Elizabeth Country Park, I made my way underneath the road to the start of Butser Hill, ready to make the climb of one of Hampshire's highest points on the chalk ridge of the South Downs. Knowing today I would be assessing all my mental and physical strength with a 6-hour hilly route, I was ready for the challenge, my mind was in the right place, and I had prepared myself for this route overnight.

Discovering it was not as bad as I had anticipated, I made my way up to the top where I could not believe the 360-degree view which was so spectacular. Suddenly I had forgotten the climb to get to the top as I simply stood and absorbed what I could see.

Suddenly, this little dog was at my feet, and it was not Samo. *"Sorry about that"* I heard this little voice, as the owner of the dog approached me. *"She is a very inquisitive dog, but she is so gentle."* I could see she was a very placid dog and Samo came over to see what all the fuss was about.

Chattering away to the owner of the dog, I told her that this was the first time I had ventured up this hill and that I could not believe the views I was seeing. I mentioned I was preparing for my South Coast Ultra Challenge in September; to raise money for Dementia UK after my nan passing away back in August 22, she seemed super excited for me.

Would you believe it though, she said that she knew the challenge that I was doing, as she had done it many years before, but now was one of the volunteers instead. She was inspirational, I am so glad that I bumped into her, it was fate, you do not realise how many people alongside you are just as nuts and crazy for taking on these amazing challenges. Such a refreshing and an uplifting conversation to send me on my way, full of positivity and strength.

As Samo and I walked down the other side of the hill, I was not prepared for how steep it would be going down, and then it suddenly hit me that I would need to prepare for going back up at some stage too. Something I had not really looked at with this route was the height of some of these hills but continued smiling and enjoying the abundance of yellow buttercups all around me. Walking around the bowl of the hill, you could see very thin footpaths making their way down to the bottom rather than it being a vertical drop which would have been a complete nightmare.

The views from here it was like someone had painted a picture with the stunning hills, one after the other, plenty of green spaces and trees, with the yellows of the rapeseed fields in the distance. A perfect blue sky with not a cloud about. Nothing looked disturbed, just pure nature as it should be, untouched.

The bushes as we made our descent were full of what looked like white elderflower as well as the pinks and yellows of the heathland and gorse. Walking through the footpath it took us through a field where the corn was right up over my waist, ready for harvesting soon.

Finally, we were arriving at our first village of Ramsden. It is one of those picturesque places where they had quaint thatched cottages, the sort of things you see down in the New Forest. We made our way past a lovely little stream running through the side of the village and headed to a local pub doing take away teas and coffees, where I sat and enjoyed a coffee and beautiful blueberry muffin before I set off once again.

Heading on to East Meon, walking through such beautiful scenery, I really was loving everything about this walk, even the hills!! Everywhere you looked was stunning, the sense of freedom and space it gave you with the sound of the birdsong and tractors in the background, so peaceful with not a sole about.

To the left of us a tractor was out ploughing ready for crops and to the right bright rapeseed with green hills in the distance and the blue skies. Where else would you want to be right now? The smell of the rapeseed was quite strong in places, especially with the heat and the slight breeze, but luckily for me I had taken my antihistamines, so I did not suffer too much.

After walking 3 hours, I started to recognise Meon Springs from many years ago. I brought Jack, my older son here when he was just a toddler, to an event where we left his favourite teddy dragon on the tractor ride.

But being the type of mum I am, to produce an idea to soothe that traumatic moment that poor Jack felt, I told him that his dragon had gone on holiday, and he was travelling around the world. This gave me a bit of time to order one on the Internet and get it back safely where he belonged. However, this was a very distinctive dragon, as he had got a bit of blue tack stuck on one of the paws and I had to try and recreate that, so he knew that it was still his dragon. I have still got that dragon now and my second son also had it as a young child, so it is an incredibly special dragon to me.

I did not realise how coming back to a place after so many years brings back those special happy memories, especially as it was just under 20 years ago!

Approaching the fisheries, stopping just after midday for a short pitstop and more refreshments, I soaked up the views of the river where there were lots of people fly fishing, as well as three elegant white swans swimming up the riverside. Heading back up the hill from the fisheries, out through the farm, I walked up a stony, and slippery flint path, which when wet was horrible, and I stood there and could not believe my eyes.

In front of me after we had passed through a kissing gate, venturing up the path were several cows just standing there, looking at me, as if to say, you are on my path, please move out the way. One black and white cow had the most beautiful heart shaped marking on its head, it was just so perfect, a real stunner. Three of them nestled into the hedgerow, whilst further up there were at least fifteen of them standing there with their eyes focused on me and Samo, and we had to make our way through, without falling in the cow pats!!

As we continued after a few kind words, they kindly moved to the side, we walked our way up quite an intense ascent of a hill till we finally got to the top. On our way up, I passed a group of 8 walkers, proper walkers, with all their backpacks and walking sticks, who were walking the whole of the South Downs Way. Well, I was impressed, and one day that is something I can achieve.

Reaching the top of this hill, we made our way along the roadway, looking over into the fields where several little lambs hopping around and feeding off their mums. There was a cute little lamb, hiding in between two trees, as if it wanted to start playing a game of peekaboo, such an epic moment.

Turning right we made our way through to Old Winchester Hill National Nature Reserve. The sign told us that *'This reserve has centuries of grazing producing the short, springy turf, rich in wildflowers, that once covered most of the South Downs. Old Winchester Hill is a relic of this now lately changed landscape.'* It was such a pretty place that I had never visited before.

Sitting there at the top of this hill with Samo, it was just starting to get a little bit misty in the bowl of the hills, but it was not long before we had the intense sun beaming on my shoulders once again.

Making our way down this ridiculously small path on the side of the hill, which was leaning quite over to the right with a reasonable drop to the side, I watched my footings to make sure I did not tumble off the track.

Approaching the bottom of this hill, going through small woodlands, we came through another gate and taking a glance as to where I was heading next, I realised the hill in front was almost vertical and the toughest one yet. Panic set in, I had been walking for hours and my legs were starting to lose their power.

Samo sat there looking at me, almost laughing to say, I have four legs, I can do this easy, and I am going to watch you struggle. At this point I thought, I am going to have to go down on my hands and knees to get to the top of this.

With perseverance and simply putting one foot in front of the other, I somehow managed to venture to the top where I discovered the Old Winchester Hill Iron Age Fort as well as an OS Trig which had been there since 1974. Certainly, worth the climb, but it assessed my strength, both mentally and physically this time. It was certainly a challenging route today.

After sitting down to regain a bit of energy, we continued further down the track, in the distance, you continued seeing beautiful green fields and then right in the middle you had a tractor in the centre of a light beige field ploughing away.

It was getting extremely hot now and we walked around the hedgerows with the App now taking us over a stile and through a field. Not sure it was the right field, as I got myself a little confused by the App, putting that down to tiredness and heat, but we continued through the fields which was not the best idea, especially when you had shorts on, and the grass was so high.

I could hardly see Samo, and the stinging nettles started biting my legs. That seemed challenging work and I am sure it would have been easier to continue the roadway around even though it was longer. However, Samo was enjoying the freedom and running through the grass, and I continued just being amazed by the views, the most beautiful views I had seen so far on my walking adventures.

Walking now for 5 hours, I was really starting to feel the heat now and looking forward to getting back on some roadway, which we eventually did as we walked up to the Sustainability Centre. Heading up the road I reached a sign which said we were walking towards Droxford, Clanfield & Hambledon and I could not believe how far we were out.

Making our way back off the road we finally set onto a flinty path, covered with overhanging trees, which was lovely to get out of the intense sun.

As we continued walking along the South Downs Way, finally in the distance I could see the Butser Kiosk, which meant we were back to where we had started. It was now just the final descent of the last hill, which I remembered the advice of a walking friend, Jane, to go down in a zigzag to take the pressure off your knees, which I did, and it helped so much, as at this point, they were feeling literally every bump and hole.

After 6.5 hours and 30km walking, I had managed to sit down and enjoy a nice, salted caramel ice cream and a refreshing can of apple juice, at The Queen Elizabeth Park Café.

A few moments after I had arrived, the walkers that I had seen up by the cows at Meon Springs had walked in. After chatting with one of them she mentioned they had come down from Yorkshire and were tackling the full South Downs Way route over 7 days.

Such a beautiful, hard walk, but totally felt a sense of accomplishment as I had battled one of my hardest routes yet.

My legs were swollen again, and my hands had started to swell which I had realised now was a walker's thing and I needed to try to shake my hands and hold them up in future walks to try to elevate some of this swelling.

Discovering not only new paths and routes I was discovering my bodies capabilities and its weaknesses. This enabled me to understand what I needed to do on future walks but for now I am absolutely loving my new paths, my new walking life and my next plan is to tackle the 100km Serpent Trail.

June 23 – 'The 100km Serpent Trail Adventures Begin'…

Part 1 - Midhurst to Petworth 20km (12 miles)

As my confidence grew, and I was exploring new routes on my own, as well as doing weekly walks with Claire, I decided I wanted to take on the Serpent Trail which was a 100.6km route that I would break down into 4 manageable sections.

Just as I was planning to start the first part of the route at the end of May I had to take a three-week course of antibiotics for a tick bite and told to avoid direct sunlight.

I was so frustrated as I had worked myself up so much to do this walk the week before, I was in the right frame of mind to take on the challenge and was so annoyed that I had this set back.

I found it extremely difficult, especially when I really got into the swing of walking on a weekly basis, but I did not let it stop me I just had to think of a way around it, and walking at night was not an option so the next plan was to simply cover up.

Hunting through Michaels selection of long cool summer shirts, I borrowed one for my adventures, making sure it was big enough to have room around me for some air flow. I hated covering up at the best of times and would rather have my shoulders uncovered so I could feel the air.

Being extremely hot on this day as well, I would have normally opted for my shorts, but I had to be sensible and put my walking trousers on. I knew I would be extremely hot, but also knew I had to compromise with myself, or put it off for 2 more weeks until my treatment had finished.

Starting the adventure 2 weeks later than planned, I walked from my home up to the top of Older Hill, which took about an hour. The heat of the sun already was getting intense, and it was only just past 10am. It was a lovely surprise to see four belted Galloways hiding under the tree for a bit of shade and the perfect start, combined with the beautiful views of the Surrey Hills.

Venturing down on this perfect summer's day, I headed towards the Duke of Cumberland Pub. I remember seeing the big serpent stone statues situated along the Serpent Trail, so I knew I was heading the right way, with my App letting me know if I ventured off the wrong way.

Walking through lots of fields I saw wonderful bright foxgloves that were out in full glow, beautiful pink ones, and you could see the bees hiding in the bells of the flower.

As I approached the Duke of Cumberland, I really needed to refuel with some ice-cold water, it was so, so hot and not even at the peak of the day. Questioning whether I had taken on too much I knew this was my last chance to get water before I reached the next pitstop at Lodsworth, a few miles off.

Hoping that someone would be in the pub as I arrived before opening time, I saw a lady outside and asked whether there was any chance of getting some ice water filled up before venturing on my way. She was so helpful, not only did she fill my bottle, but she also gave me a pint glass of fresh ice-cold water that went down so well. So pleased I stopped here.

Walking through a dried mud track that obviously in parts was regularly prone to flooding, I crossed a small wooden bridge. The area was pretty with hundreds of ferns shooting new leaves and lines of pine trees, with the sunshine glimpsing through, providing shelter as I walked.

Such a beautiful walk, which then took you up towards Bexley Hill and again, with stunning rows of foxgloves. When you got to the top, you had these little peak holes that you could see further into the distance of Surrey Hills, and I managed to get some amazing photos. Although it was quite a climb to the top when you looked out at the spectacular views, you soon forget the hard climb and started making your way down the other side, it was quite a relief.

Heading now towards Lodsworth, walking on the public footpath over one of the local farmers fields, I was into Lodsworth, and I diverted from my route to pop into The Lodsworth Larder, the local village shop, where I stocked up with two bottles of water and a nice can of cold coke. Grabbing a freshly made tasty sandwich, I sat in the shaded area, whilst I recharged my slightly flattened battery. I am so glad I did not bring Samo on this route as it was far too hot.

Today though I knew it was appropriate training for September, my 1st Ultra Marathon Challenge, and I had to be ready just in case it was extremely hot temperatures like today. I believe so far today, it was one of the hottest days we had had so far this year and I had certainly picked the wrong day as it was not particularly fun walking in such heat, and it certainly slowed down my pace.

My next part of the trail was heading towards Upperton, and I remember getting into some coverings with another cool water stream running through it. Again, this was quite comforting to have that shade again, but I was soon back out in the heat, where I approached the top of Petworth Park, heading back into Upperton and Tillington. It was nice to see the sign to somewhere that I was familiar with and knew that I would be heading over into Petworth very soon for my lift back home to Midhurst.

My feet were really starting to suffer now and blister up as the heat was becoming too hot. It really was testing to be walking in that sort of heat but all good practice I suppose. I was feeling slightly drained and took cover under the Conker tree down at the pavilion for a little bit, just so I could recover a bit.

Heading towards the village of Tillington, I then walked by the side of the church and started heading up the main road, on the pathway through to Petworth. The blooms that had come out, as you entered Petworth were spectacular.

You could see the alliums, the foxgloves, and a range of other brightly coloured flowers. There were pinks, white, yellows and blues, it looked fantastic.

Finally, my last bit of the route was walking down to Hampers Green because I wanted to get down to where my parents lived, so I could get a lift back home to Midhurst, and such a relief when I saw their front door.

My legs were on fire. For the first time on this walk, I had experienced what they call Disney Rash, or Walker's rash, where my legs halfway up my shins where swollen and covered in bright red markings, looking like someone had poured boiling water over my legs.

Blistering had come up on my feet and on some parts of my legs as well. I had quite a few blotchy marks over my feet and now I was a bit concerned.

From Yoga I had remembered having my legs up the wall to help with the circulation and to stop the swelling in my legs. So, I did this after I had a soak in a cooling bath with Epsom Salts, something else I had found beneficial.

Such an achievement though, I had completed the first part of the Serpent Trail, and in total that one was just under 20km taking me just over 5.5 hours of walking which in that heat was extremely good going. It is one that I would like to redo again but when it is not so hot.

'The Serpent Trail continues'.

Part 2 - Petworth to Midhurst - 23km (14 miles)

Venturing out on my second part of the Serpent Trail the following week, the trail started from Petworth over to Flexham Park, on to Fittleworth, through to Lord's Piece, up to Heathend, and then crossing over to Duncton Common and walking to Graffham over the Heyshott Roughs and back into Midhurst. It was a slightly longer route than the week that I had done before, in fact, it took me just over 6 hours, showing up as just over 23 km on my App.

The day started off quite cloudy, in comparison to the week before, where it had been beaming sunshine. As I walked down over the Sheepdowns a place that I had not been since I was in my teens, memories of my childhood flooded back. We often used to cut though into town this way when I lived at Hampers Green.

I never remembered it being such an extremely long hill down and up though. Greeted by many horses roaming freely in the fields, a big brown horse with such a stern look, stared at me and beside him was a beautiful white horse that looked like it could have been a unicorn, simply missing its horn.

They were very, very calm and did not come over, just munched on the grass, happy in their surroundings. I did not obviously have the dog with me again on such a long route, which was also handy as walking through a field with 10 or 12 horses in, I am not sure what he would have been like.

The sky darkened over by the time I had reached Flexham Park, and I did wonder if I was going to get soaked by the rain today so luckily had my waterproof coat with me just encase.

Discovering an old farm trailer that had been sitting in the fields for many years rusted out, I continued the route until I came across these beautiful little chocolate box houses, with thatched roofs and Tudor style fronts as I made my way into Little Bignor. Such a pretty and quaint little place.

Heading up into Fittleworth, I stopped in the new Village Store, which I did not realise was there, it is a long time ago since I had been here. I enjoyed a delicious slice of rocky road and a coffee to keep me going, topping up with a Lucozade Sport, as they were always refreshing and gave you that much needed boost of energy as you walked.

Walking past The Swan Pub, which I have many fond memories of as a young girl, it seemed so derelict and hidden by the scaffolding. I crossed over the bridge, as I walked up the pathway alongside the road, it had started raining, so the paths were starting to get muddy, wet and a bit slippery.

Next, I discovered I was at Lords Piece, a place I had heard of many times but had never visited. The views where amazing, very sandy to walk on and full of ferns and heathland. Carrying on following the route, walking past Sutton End house, I remember smiling and thinking to myself, I cannot believe I have got this far yet again on a new route.

I was so excited and pleased with myself, I was yet again on a new adventure and enjoying the experience of just being in my own company, which is something I have always struggled with before.

As I continued, I came to the most amazing set of ponds, at Burton Mill. It was utterly amazing, so peaceful and tranquil with not a soul about. The waterfalls that whereby the side of me, where you could stop and listen as the water trickled down, whilst you glanced at the vibrant flowers, it was a perfect place to be.

Heading out of the woods out through further fields, walking past more horses, I headed out towards Heathend and crossed the road to the local farm shop.

The sun had come out again and it was getting very warm, so being lunchtime, I stopped for a bag of crisps and a refueling drink and a sandwich, as I was not sure if there would be any more stops till I got back to Midhurst. I started to go on for the next part of my adventure and walked past a garden which had these amazing sculptures, wooden carved horses, made of driftwood. They were stunning and thought they would sit lovely in our garden back home!

Certainly, a woodland walk as I continued through more woods taking me into Duncton Common which I had walked parts of before. As I approached Lavington Plantation full of beautiful trees, so tall and spindly. I read a sign that said:

"This area was open heathland until 1958, when it was planted with Scots pine trees. There were concerns about a future timber shortage and Scots pine grow well in sandy, low nutrient soil, so large areas of heathland were densely planted with trees. This land was gifted to The National Trust in 2000 with the aim of restoring the heath and all its wildlife."

Their restoration plans were certainly working as there was so much wildlife to discover; the stonechat, nightjar, and woodlark as well as the common lizards and adders, which I certainly did not want to bump into, as I do not like snakes.

Carrying on I come across more Serpent Stones, so I knew I was on the right route. I made my way into Graffham Common greeted with such fresh and fragrant beautiful pink rhododendrons, plus more of the woods and heathland.

Walking through a big, gated section, I came across more sculptures, but these were slightly different, carved from stone I believe, which comprised of a little pig with a lamb on the top of it, a random discovery.

As I ventured deeper into the heathland, heading into the Heyshott Roughs, I walked through trails leading me through beautiful vibrant yellow gorse bushes which where lovely to look at but not to walk past, as they were sharp and would scratch your arms.

So many twisted old remains of trees too, something with which I am always fascinated. I love looking at the way that they grow, and they twist, and they lean on each other, and they sprout out in new directions. It is just incredible the way that happens that they can break off in parts, yet continue in a different direction, full of life.

Finally, I was coming into the last part of the route, walking back up by the Kennels Dairy, it was almost 3pm and I needed to pick up the pace to get back to the car park where I had planned to meet my dad for a lift back to Petworth.

Once again as I untaped my feet when I got home, they were blotchy, and my legs really swollen again. I had blistered this time too and knew I really had to take my walking seriously now and invest in my footwear, because I really was in tune with this walking and really enjoying it. I did not want the blisters to stop me from walking, so that evening I made that purchase of my first proper set of Walking Boots ready for my next adventure.

'The Serpent Trail continues again'.

Part 3 - Midhurst to Petersfield - 16km (10 miles)

After walking on smaller routes over the week to wear in my new walking boots, today I was going to embark on the third part of the Serpent Trail. After dropping Harry at school, I started making my way from home up to The Country Inn at Bepton, to grab my regular coffee and cookie to get me going.

The sun was beaming down already, and I made my way through Iping Common, heading out towards Elsted which I had walked several times over the last few weeks, so knew where I was heading.

The forecast showed it was going to be a sweltering day with showers later this afternoon, so hopefully I would make my way to Petersfield before the heavens opened. This meant that the paths were nice and dry, and I was certainly getting quite used to this after walking through so much rain during the Winter. It really does make it different walking when you have not got to straddle the muddy puddles.

As I walked through a row of very tall, uniformed pine trees I followed the signs of the Serpent Trail, which then took me through the common, consisting of beautiful dark and light pink heathers and lots of greenery. It was a heathland walk this morning so far.

Climbing one of the smaller hills at Elsted Common, I stopped to admire the beautiful blue skies and the views around me. Not a cloud in the sky, with soft golden sandy paths, which Samo always loved when I brought him over this way. Today again I left him at home as it was far too hot and long to be venturing out.

Butterflies, so many butterflies on this route. I was forever crossing the paths of these wonderful, winged insects. So many of the Red Admirals, the Large Whites and what looked like the Brown Hairstreaks flying around the paths.

The footpath leads me through a field full of the rapeseed pods and amongst the pods you saw a glimpse of more beautiful butterflies and bright red poppies. I could feel my cheeks glowing on fire as it was really starting to get hot now or was this simply the menopause giving me a hot flush. I could never tell the difference these days.

Walking over a bridge I continued walking up onto a road walking past the Southdowns Manor, before heading through to Nyewood, where I came across a Wood Carving Studio.

The only reason I knew it was this was because outside the entrance they had this humongous, what looked like a peanut shape piece of wood with the 'Wood Carving Studio' carved out of it.

From Nyewood, I continued to walk through fields of golden oats which was as tall as my shoulders! Walking past someone's garden, to make my way on to the next part of the trail, there was an incredible tree in the distance. It looked like it had been hit by lighting at some point, just pure smooth bark, no leaves just the amazing sculpture that it had left.

Walking further through Nyewood, with Marbled White butterflies flying to one side of me I came across a fantastic wooden chicken, carved out on the fence post to the entrance of a house on the other side.

I walked past an incredibly old tractor which was buried in the hedge and looked like it had been there for over 30 years. The hedge had grown around it, as well as through it, and now was a place that is used for storing cut logs.

Discovering next the Cemex West Heath Quarry, a place I never knew existed until today. It is amazing when you start walking that you discover so many unfamiliar places and areas you would never see by driving.

Passing over some waterways, I took a detour to another favourite stop 'The Tea Barn at Durleighmarsh. A perfect excuse to sit and enjoy a slice of rocky road and a coffee with a refreshing apple juice to finish off. This was often a place I would plan into my route when I started walking The Durleighmarsh Circular.

So far, I had been walking for just over 3 hours and had about another hour to go, but I knew this part of the route, so I relaxed and enjoyed it as I knew there were no hills or surprises to come. On this route I had been lucky as it had been flat which was a change, as the last few weeks seemed to have been full of hilly experiences.

Crossing over the main road I once again headed on the footpath this time walking through a field of unripe wheat, again was as tall as your shoulders. Passing through a small farm I then walked onto the next field which I love, as it has the most stunning large oak tree right in the middle of it. I do not know what it is, simply its placement in the field, or it is grand presence that makes it a handsome tree.

Daisies were everywhere in the field as I walked across to the next kissing gate, which would take me on a small bridge to head over a small river, where I reached several free roaming cows in this wetland part of the route.

They were not the belted Galloway's which I always was bumping into, but they were of the cow variety so that had made my walk! I am a sucker for cows, I love them. There is something magical about them, all their inquisitiveness and funny faces especially when they stick their large tongues out as you attempt to take a selfie.

Coming up to 12.30pm I was heading up to Petersfield Heath and it was just starting to darken with black rain clouds so hopefully I can get back to the car in time. Michael had taken the car to his work so I could drive it home and pop back and pick him up later when he had finished.

Approaching Petersfield Lake just after 1pm, I was greeted by what seemed hundreds of noisy geese and ducks. You could see the Egyptian geese with their little red feet and some of them came over to me as I sat on the bench for a while, just enjoying my achievement of walking the third part of the Serpent Trail back over to Petersfield.

This walk was certainly the easiest part of the Serpent Trail, and I knew I had left the harder part till next week, where I would have to take on the challenge of walking from Haslemere back to Midhurst via Rake. It took me just over 4 hours to do this walk today and it was about 16km in total, and I was quite impressed with this route.

Not a lot of hills, quite a flat route, with a combination of road and woodlands, sandy areas, which made it a lot easier than the previous parts of the Serpent Trail routes. Looking forward to next week when I can hopefully complete the final part!

'The Serpent Trail Finale'

Part 4 - Haslemere to Midhurst - 46km (28 miles)

Saving the best to last, that is what they say, well for me, this was saving the hardest part to last. I knew this was going to be the longest bit of the trail and I had been putting it off until I was in the right headspace to take it on as I knew it was going to be a tough trail and could not do it half-heartedly.

I caught the bus up to Haslemere after I dropped Harry at school, and when I arrived at the bus station, I would start to walk through the town and get to my starting point, which on the Alltrails app was at Swan Barn Farm. It was an area that covered around thirty hectares and supported a variety of wildlife within its semi ancient woodland, hedgerows, pasture and hay meadows, an orchard and several streams and ponds.

Never realising that such a beautiful little place could exist in a small town. Off I went venturing though this beautiful area, heading up through the woodlands where there were very, very tall, high pine trees. It was such a beautiful blue day again and I had been so lucky with the weather.

The sun was shining, and I came across the first gated entrance, which took me onto The Serpent Trail. I headed to Blackdown Forest, another National Trust place of interest.

Forgetting just how amazing the views were from the top as I had not been here for many years, I walked looking through the gap of the trees. All you could see in the distance were views of beautiful countryside that just seemed to go on for miles and miles. The views really were breathtaking.

I remember standing there and just absorbing the view for quite a while, and then I could hear this rustling behind me. As I turned around, to my surprise and happiness I saw several belted Galloways roaming the woods, which is now becoming a regular thing I see on my walks.

This one had leant across a big tree root and was trying to reach up again, like the giraffe, trying to get the vegetation from the top of the trees. You could see a few more too, hiding behind the trees and the hedgerows with their bold black and white markings.

I continued walking through the beautiful area of the Temple of the Winds, taking in the overwhelming views of luscious green trees and ferns that you could see for miles. I took on quite some stony paths and this obviously was a popular area because I did bump into a lot of dog walkers.

It was an area with so many different intertwining routes, but I followed the one on my App, which then took me through fields, and I remember seeing these beautiful bright pink thistles that had these stunning orange butterflies on them.

Heading on now to Valewood Park, again, another National Trust area, I walked past what I call the giant rhubarb leaves. Every time I see these, it really does bring back some special memories for me, of my dad and brother and summer times at Ramster Gardens, where during the school holidays, when we were very small, my dad was doing building work there and we would play in a little caravan doing colouring, looking over the big pond that had these huge rhubarb leaves!

As I continued down a pathway that had been prone to flooding, I came across a raised wooden walkway, looking at these incredible fungi on the sides of the bark of the trees next to me. This one had looked like a spaceship had been thrown into the side of a tree.

The birds singing and chirping away, and I made my way down some steps to a natural small pond to the side of me, a very tranquil and peaceful place, very undisturbed. I had looked down and saw the little snails enjoying the fresh leaves and dampness from the pond.

Approaching Fernden Heights I made my way over the main road at Marley Hangar where I then ventured up at this point, quite a high hill, which looked like you were going through the back between two people's gardens. It was a tough hill to try and make your way up, with steep little steps which certainly pulled on every leg muscle.

I had been walking just under 2.5 hours, and so had done quite a trek already. Luckily, I had my waterproofs with me because the heavens truly opened, and it started pouring down with rain. I was under a bit of cover heading through the woods, before coming out at another junction to Lynch, Fernhurst and Linchmere church. I continued through more woodlands where I came across a perfect little den that someone had made in the woods.

Next on my trail I came up to North Lodge Farm, and then I seemed to appear on a track of another golf course. Following the old tractor doing its green maintenance, I checked it was safe to walk and there were no flying golf balls. I really did not want to be hit by one of those. After making my way through the golf course, I continued to richer heathland, which everywhere you looked were stunning purple heathers.

Knowing soon that my next check point was Rake Garden Centre, I marched on ready to get a much-needed sandwich to refuel as I was starting to flag now. I had been walking for 5 hours as it was just coming up to 2pm and I knew it was still a long way home. So, after I had refreshed myself with food and drink and a change of socks as my feet had got quite wet, I headed back off to try to get home before 6pm when Michael would be back.

I found myself firstly at Rake Hanger and read a sign, which told me it was *'an ancient woodland that has been covered in trees since at least 1600 AD. Of course, the individual trees are less than four hundred years old because the new ones have grown up to replace them as they die.'* An incredibly special, enchanted little place that is a hidden little gem that you do not see from the roadside.

As I walked through the woodland, I could feel a little niggle under my foot and I thought, I am sure a bit of my tape's come ajar, but I persevered, and I continued. Once I started walking again, although something was irritating me, I choose to continue as I did not feel at this time it was enough to make me stop at this point.

I continued down through some fields till I came up to track, which by the side of a gate, someone had created an amazing brightly painted wooden totem pole with five heads and these big horns, it was fantastic and what an entrance to a house.

Approaching the next field, it was perfectly baled and ready to be collected. The bales were all wrapped up in their black plastic wrapping, and so uniformed in the way they were dropped, that obviously the tractor could then just come and pick them up all in lines.

Overhead I saw the most stunning buzzard flying and I knew it was not a kite because I had looked for its forked tail and could not see it. I managed to get a fantastic photo of it with its wings split and could see it was definitely not a beautiful Red Kite.

Making my way now through more thick heathlands and woodlands, I approached Bull Hill where I had often from the roadway seen that the bikes would be flying down these jumps, hills, and mud tracks. Something luckily, they were not doing today as I was walking through the top of the route. They must have nerves of steel to ride these tracks as the drops down to the other side are terrifying, well for me they are.

Heading now to Terwick Common, Borden Wood and Kingsham Wood, I was trekking through one woodland to another before finally reaching Titty Hill at Stedham which I had discovered before on a smaller route close to home.

As I made my way down the hill through a vast area of tall pine trees, the ground was slippery and at the bottom making my way through the field to a gate, it took me on the home straight, but it was so boggy. How I did not sink in that part I do not know. You could tell the cows had been there recently too due to the flies and deposits they had left.

As I ventured from Titty Hill back on to the top of Eastshaw Lane I finally knew that the upcoming Woolbeding bridge was near and only a short distance from home. I was really starting to suffer with my feet at this time, but obviously knew I had no option but to go on. I think it did not help as I knew I was near to home and as soon as you get that point in your head I always started to struggle. I find it much easier to walk into the unknown as you take each part of the challenge with fresh energy.

I had been walking for almost 9 hours, and it had shown me 46 km on my Fitbit. That was about the same distance that I would be doing when I was doing my first challenge in September. I was shattered and had an extremely, huge sore blister on the underside of my foot.

This at times became unbearable to walk on, as it went across the whole of my foot, but I was so proud of myself as I had done it and, I was confident that I could embark on completing that Ultra Marathon now.

I did pay the price afterwards on this walk because I did not listen to that niggle on the bottom of my feet at the halfway point. I learnt the hard way, as for 2 weeks after I was walking around with a homemade donut under my foot, that I had remembered how to do from Red Cross when I was a child.

I had to stop walking for a couple of weeks to let my foot recover, as it was important that my feet were at the strongest point now because it was only 7 weeks away till my challenge in September.

But it was a lesson well learnt that has helped me so much on future walks and it has shown me how much strength and resilience I have. I discovered that when you want something so much, you do find that inner strength for somewhere. At times I thought about giving up and taking the easy option and calling for a lift home, but I dug deep and continued.

Completion of that 100km over those four weeks has been such a fantastic achievement. In fact, with my few wrong turns along the way I was a bit over the 100.6km route you would do if you did it in one hit. How people can do it all in one go, I do not know, but in years to come, that is something I can embark on when I have been walking for longer and I am a lot stronger and fitter. I forget that I am only months into my recovery still.

So, if you are ever up that way and you have an opportunity to do the Serpent Trail, whether it is parts of it, or all in one go, then do, it is a wonderful experience with so many amazing views.

June 23 – 'The Marina Walk'

Chichester Marina and Dell Quay Circular - 18km (11 miles)

Becoming braver to venture out further with my adventures, I discovered a route on my Alltrails App which took me on a circular route from Chichester Marina heading through to St Peter's Place, Fishbourne Meadows, Bosham and Itchenor ending up at Birdham Pool before heading back to the start.

Being out amongst the harbour basin, sounded like the perfect walk seeing different views from my normal fields and woodlands. It even entailed a boat ride halfway from one side of the harbour to the other to make the complete circular route.

As I set out the sun was pitching through already, the skies where blue and there was a lot of activity going on at the marina already, the perfect day for walking.

Thank God I had finished my antibiotics as I did not have to cover up completely again, knowing it was going to get hot today. I had become extremely cautious though about where I walked now as the bite was not something I wanted to get again as it was a horrible bite, and I had a nasty reaction.

Starting out at the marina after grabbing a coffee to start me on my way, the views out to the harbour and into the marina with the hundreds of boats and yachts, all moored up by their pontoons, was so impressive. I headed over the harbour lock and made my way onto the footpath which took me on the outskirts of the marina with its beautiful wildlife and meadow flowers.

Walking on further around the footpath, whilst catching glimpses of the harbour with its broken trees and driftwood by the water's edge, I approached a bench nestled in high luscious green grass followed by a meadow full of bright pink flowers and yellow buttercups. Heading then through a field where the rape had stopped flowering, the pods were starting to show ready for the next stage for harvesting.

I headed over next through Dell Quay with the old wooden boats balanced up against the wall and I set off down a long wooden slatted pathway as I headed into the Fishbourne Meadows. Venturing off route to see the dinky little church called St Peter's place, a robin flew in front of my pathway, so I knew I was in good company.

Heading back over the meadows which according to the sign placed at the start of the meadow walk, *'These beautiful meadows were once part of the Roman Harbour, linked to Fishbourne Roman Palace (c1AD), and are protected as a Scheduled Ancient Monument and a Site of Nature Conservation Importance'*.

Walking by the side of a clear chalk water stream, fenced off to protect the growing number of water voles, I then made my way through a field with reeds higher than my head. There was a narrow pathway right through the middle of it and then hidden was a small bridge to cross over another slightly faster and higher stream, before heading back on to a road where I discovered a large patch of the famous large rhubarb I had seen on previous walks.

I arrived at Fletchers Place where I walked past a set of beautiful cottages which were rich in bright red rambling roses before making my way to the Bosham to Itchenor Footpath Ferry.

That boat was so refreshing with the breeze of the water as we sped over to the other side of the harbour. As soon as I got off to the pontoon, I walked my way up to a small café a few minutes away to grab a cooling drink, and a bite to eat too, as it was lunchtime. From there I headed back around Itchenor making my way to the breathtaking Birdham Pool. The houses around the waterways were amazing, so grand and unique and with such beautiful large prestigious gardens. I could imagine living here that is for sure.

As I reached Birdham Pool there were so many friendly swans that came over to the water's edge letting me take photos of them and then elegantly swimming off leaving ripples behind them.

Finally making my way on the last bit part of the route back to the start, I discovered the houseboats on the side of a disused canal, full of water lilies with dragonflies flying over the water. I had walked for just over 3.5 hours, and just over 18km and as the walk is so peaceful and beautiful I have continued to walk it a few times since.

One thing I learnt is that you just have check that the boat is running beforehand as there is nothing like walking halfway round, to realise you must head back to the start and head in the other direction to do the full walk! But that is another story....

July 23 – 'The Walk of The Hare'

SDW Cocking to Arundel 28km (17 miles)

Some walks you really do enjoy, and I must say that the SDW walk that I did back in July, walking from the top of Cocking Hill across to Amberley and Arundel was one of those most memorable walks I have done. 28km in 5.5 hours over hills, flinty paths and views that went for miles, was the perfect way to see the downs for me.

Setting out quite early in the morning, it started off dark wet and grey, but with the hope that the weather was going to get warmer come midday I enjoyed the start of a fantastic walk over the downs.

Today I really needed this walk as it had been a couple of weeks since Grandad was taken into Rotherlea Care Home as he was more unstable at home and needed the 24-hour care. Such a challenging time for everyone, seeing him in a place that he did not want to be but for his own health and safety it was the right decision, but a decision that I felt so guilty about.

Using todays walk as a therapy session to help process what was going on, I headed up on the roadway, rather than up the long-wet grass to the side of Cocking Hill, as I did not really want to get soaked feet within the first 10 minutes.

I continued up the hill and turning right heading up past Richline Farm, I walked up a quite muddy and slippery route, which improved the higher up the hill I got. It was the perfect spot to see the sunrise, which was always such a brilliant way to start any walk and a good reason to get your walking boots on early.

As the sun broke through, I managed to take fantastic photos of the views, as well as trying to capture the rare sighting of 2 brown hares running at the top of the hill. It was only 30 minutes into my walk too, and I thought this is going to be a fantastic walk, feeling so positive and full of energy seeing this wonderful wildlife so early on.

It was incredibly quiet for the first hour of my trek but then as I approached a part of the downs just passing the crossroads sign to East Lavington, Cocking and East Dean the walkers began to appear. I thought they had the same idea as me today but looked more equipped and serious walkers and they were doing the whole of the South Downs Way, a route I am still working my way through.

This route so far was a bit unsteady underfoot and hard to walk on in places, due to it being full of flint and chalk pathways, but such stunning views of the fields and hills in the distance along the way made it manageable. Coming down to the Upwaltham straight and heading over the road into another fielded area, I had discovered my happy cows and sheep which always brightened my day. The sun kept coming out and then hiding away by the darkened clouds, so it was a very mixed bag today, but so stuffy at the same time, maybe a thunderstorm was brewing.

My coat permanently was on and off, liked it was on all my walks now. I think with the EDS (Ehler Danlos Syndrome) that I suffer with, it gives me more problems regulating my temperature, which to be honest, I always thought was just to do with the Raynaud's, and even the menopause at times. It just makes it more frustrating with the walking as I can change from minute to minute and find it difficult when choosing what to wear so I do not freeze or boil over.

By midday it had turned hot, the clouds had disappeared, and it was the perfect summers day with blue skies and beautiful sunshine. I discovered a memorial stone which had the name 'Toby' from 1888 to 1955. It said, *"Here he lies where he longed to be. Home is the sailor home from the sea and the hunter home from the hill."*

Such a moving war memorial and something that I often discovered on my walks, where memorials either from the war times, or simply memorial benches of loved ones that had spent their times enjoying the South Downs Way.

Carrying on I came to a massive log stack, where they had been cutting down trees before looking over into the distance and seeing Amberley and the river below. I could not believe already I was at this point. I had seen markers along the way of a walking or cycling event and then as I came to the main road, three push bikers had stopped repairing their wheels. I gathered the event was for bikes and I am glad I had walked that part already, so I did not have to keep stopping to let them go by.

Preplanning for Michael to pick me up from Amberely, I phoned him to say I had a change of plan and asked could he pick me up from Arundel, as I thought because I had previously done the walk from Amberley to Arundel, I could extend my route and complete a further few km to add to my training plan.

I had certainly conquered several hills today and my legs were getting tired, at this point, I was 4 hours into my route. I looked down at the hill which I had to make my way down to get to the river before venturing back to Arundel and it was super steep.

I remembered the zigzag walk Jane had advised me to use previously to help with my knees and stability. I put that into action, and it helped especially with the loose flint underfoot. I needed to be careful, as I certainly did not want to get an injury here so close to my event day. The views making my way down, went for miles and I was so pleased with myself for making it so far, in such wonderful time as well. I ventured back the way I had done on the previous route I did with Claire back in March 23, and headed by The Black Rabbit, carrying on into Arundel and finishing at the Café, where I knew the coffee was great and so was their shortbreads.

Such a beautiful walk, where you could see spectacular views of the Downs, and it will certainly be one of my most favourite walks to walk again. Next time I will start in Arundel and make my way back to Cocking, however I know how hard that hill would be in reverse from Amberley to the top of Bury Hill! So will leave it to a day I have super hill abilities. Today this really did help as by the time I had finished my walk I had felt so much better about Grandads care package. We knew the next few months would be difficult as we would be going on this journey with him, try to help him find his way and make this new place a home. Overtime this would happen, but we needed to all give it time and let him adjust, visiting daily when I could and calling also to make sure he was ok.

July 23 – 'The Inquisitive Horse Walk'

Welldiggers, Hesworth & Fittleworth Circular 9km (5.5 miles)

Summer is truly here, and I started to tie routes close to Petworth in with seeing my grandad at Rotherlea Nursing Home. Parking at the Welldiggers Arms, I walked the circular route around Hesworth Common and Fittleworth, into Little Bignor and back to the start. It is always such a short pretty 9km walk.

It was an extremely sweltering day, so heading out in my shorts and t-shirt, dosing myself in suncream, I set off reaching a beautiful little Church at Egdean hidden away from the main road.

After taking a little peak at the church I headed over to the main road, crossing over and walking down a little lane before taking the footpath through two fields where six or seven horses were grazing.

Panicking a little as I had Samo with me, and I did not know how they would react to him, I walked into the field and the horses marched over towards where we were walking.

I remember walking faster and faster because I did not want the horses to get to close to us and was relieved to get to the other side of the gate. They were just making sure we got out of their field, even though it was a public footpath.

There was a beautiful white horse that came over to us at first, but it was a bit of a hair-raising moment as they all were so inquisitive, thought we had food. But they soon lost interest and walked off back to grazing in their field.

Heading now up a twisting lane, I made my way over into Hesworth Common. I never realised that the common was so big and had so many different paths and hills, but so pretty, full of colourful heathers everywhere.

As I made my way to the top of another hill, again it is one of those hills that does not look too bad, but once you start walking, you do get out of breath at times. I finally reached the top and discovered a bench where I could take 5 minutes to recuperate.

I did wonder about snakes because I had seen in previous social media posts to be careful where you are walking, but touch wood, we have been lucky so far on all the walks and not seen a snake.

Walking out of the common and walking up an alleyway the opposite side of the road, towards the school, I wandered past a house, and in the wall was a little face, looking at me. Progressing up by the wall there were more of them as well as a fantastic metal sculpture of a cow or horse's head. Those little ceramic screwed up faces, something creepy but fascinating at the same time.

Approaching the new Fittleworth Village shop, it was the perfect stop for a flapjack and a coffee. One thing I always try to plan in my routes, is a decent pit stop as when you are walking, you need to keep refueling. Not the best thing with a coffee and a flapjack, but it is what got me through all my walks so far.

After having a 10 – 15 minute breather, I continued over the road and walked across to a lovely little smallholding. Seeing little pigs, sheep, and chickens, 'happy as larry' in their little field, was such a welcome surprise.

Heading up now through some woods, I then walked down some steep steps into Little Bignor such a pretty village with its dainty little chocolate box houses. Stopping and talking to one of the gentlemen who lived in the houses, attending to his garden roses, he asked where I was walking today.

I explained that I was training for my first ever Ultra Marathon in memory of my nan and raising money for Dementia UK. He was really, really inspired by what I was doing and wished me all the luck and success and to continue doing the excellent work that I was doing for others. Something so special about when people unknown to you are interested in what you are doing, and it always gives me a bit of a buzz as well.

Walking through the fields heading back towards the starting point, there were golden glowing crops ready to be harvested very soon. The fields were beaming with bright red poppies hidden within the crop and such a perfect picture moment with the fields, the views, blue skies, and poppies.

Taking just over 2 hours, and around the 9km mark, if you have ever got a couple of hours and you want to go somewhere and just refresh and gather your thoughts, it is always one of the popular smaller ones that I turn back to when I have got a couple of hours.

It is a lovely little walk, which has small climbs to get your heart pounding. You can also extend the route a little bit, depending on which path you want to take when you get to Hesworth Common, but highly recommended this route.

We are incredibly lucky to have these little routes. Not all the walks need to be a massive six-hour ones. I love doing the long walks, but I have realised I do not need to be doing the long walks all the time.

You get as much reward and satisfaction in doing smaller routes too, whether it is 1 hour, 2 hours, half an hour, it is just being out in nature and appreciating what we've have around us which matters. If you can get out in all the different seasons too, and different weathers, rather than just walking in the same weather in the same place, you really see and experience such different things.

We are so, so lucky to live in the heart of the South Downs and have all these incredible places to walk. I love now exploring, and having the courage to take on routes that I never did before. Those times when I have looked at a different path, a path I have walked past repeatedly, wondering where it goes and eventually being brave enough to take that risk and going for it, because you never know where it is going to lead.

I am always under the opinion that if you go down a path and it really is that bad, you either turn around and come back or you continue, but you just do not add it on your next list of ones to revisit. Luckily, I do not think out of all the walks I have done to date, I have ever had one that has been that bad that I would not go back on.

There are certainly ones that are more enjoyable than others, but that is purely also to do with your frame of mind and where you are in the day, with what is going on. Times can be hard, and sometimes walks can be harder.

Some days you can walk for miles and miles and other days, you feel like just doing a mile is too much, but what I have found for me is that once you step out, after 10 minutes of walking when you think you can't do it, your mind changes, nature has been helping me, it has healed me on days I needed healing.

Never give up, never think that is it, I hate walking, I am not doing it again. If you did not enjoy that one, do not do it again, put it down to an experience, all walks are different. Just because you had a rough walk, do not give up and think all walks are now going to be bad. It is an off day, we all have them, and you start a new day, as the sun rises, and you put back on your walking boots and start again with a new adventure.

Every day I put my walking boots on I get excited about what I will see as I start a new adventure.

August 23 - 'The Walk of the Rings'

Washington, Cissbury & Chanctonbury Ring - 20km (12 miles)

August 23 my adventures took me today on a different adventure over the downs which was a lovely change to the normal routes I had been repeating. Looking on my Alltrails App I found a circular route heading from Washington up to Cissbury Ring, and Chanctonbury Ring and back to the start. I thought that it would be great practice as I knew next month I would be covering some of this route in my Ultra Challenge.

It was approx. a 20 km walk and took me about 4 hours to complete, starting off parking at a bottom of a hill near a pub, where I walked through a small field and up quite an incline of a hill. It was a beautiful warm day and not the type of day for walking up hills, and it certainly had a few hills today, that is for sure. Once you made it to the top though and saw those views you were completely rewarded.

Reaching the top of one hill, Samo and I then made our way over to another, Chanctonbury Hill, full of free roaming cows, which was quite exciting and nice to see because if you know me by now, I have a love for cows.

I blame that on my grandad, being a dairy farmer for a lot of his life. These cows were just wandering around the top, munching on the leaves from the trees, and the fresh grass all around the top of the hill.

You had to watch where you were walking though because they were huddled all together, there were about fifty cows, but it was a unique experience seeing them so close and their funny little expressions.

We made our way back down that hill then across the top of the downs until we ventured across to Cissbury Ring. As we got to the top of this high climb the clouds came over, but it was so, so muggy, and another one of my adventures that my coat was on and off, but no wet feet today so far!

It was a fantastic route, where you could see for miles and miles. It was a regular walking route for people, the paths were very worn, and I could almost see Brighton and Littlehampton in the distance too.

I remember seeing a lot of those red and orange berried plants, Lords and Ladies, out in full bloom so was careful where the dog went, as I knew these were poisonous. I then came across what looked like Canterbury Bells, the beautiful purple belled flowers, and many types of mushrooms to. Remarkably interesting seeing different plants, and wildlife as well as different views and such fun discovering somewhere new to walk.

Combining was going on in the background too, and the dust that was coming off the fields in the distance. I came across a huge combine sat in the field, whether it had broken down, or the farmer had finished for the day, I did not know. I continued walking through lots of yellow fields, in the cloudy skies, with green trees and made my way back along the downs to the trail that I had picked up initially at the start.

So, refreshing seeing these new dramatic views, and it gave me the inspiration to keep on looking further afield and discover new routes in the future.

September 23 – 'My First Ultra Marathon for Dementia UK'

Hove to Arundel - 42km (26 miles)

The night before and the nerves really started to set in! What have I done, it is my first ever Ultra Marathon, am I mad? I am sure most people would enter a simple marathon for their first event and then work themselves up to an Ultra Marathon! Well, if you do not know me by now you have realised that I do not do things by halves, when I set my mind on doing something I want to do it!

I was meant to be walking over twenty-six miles tomorrow, and I am now questioning myself. How am I going to do that? It has been so hot this week and tomorrow is forecast to be the same, how am I going to make it through??

These were all the thoughts going through my head right now as I am starting to pack my bags to make sure I have everything I need. Laying everything on the bed I made sure that I had ticked everything off the checklist: plasters, painkillers, KT tape, food, water, head torch and everything else that you could think of to get you through apart from the kitchen sink!

Somehow, I managed to pack it into the smallest rucksack I could find as I wanted to go with the least weight as possible!

Alarm set for 3.30am and off to bed for an early night (after I had made my overnight porridge laden with nuts, seeds, and fruit ready for the morning), I had to make sure I had a decent night's sleep ready for my adventures tomorrow.

Setting off at 4.30am, Michael kindly took me down to Hove Football Ground ready for my 6am start. I said, *"I'll see you when I see you,"* as I had no idea how long it was going to take. This was my first ever challenge and I did not even know if I would finish, but I was going to give it everything I had. I am nervous and really, really excited at the same time. I had put an awful lot of effort into training for the event so should be ok.

 I had picked up my starter kit and my number, 6052, and it was all becoming very real now as I pinned my number on my rucksack figuring out where the best place was to pin it. I was experiencing my first ever Ultra Marathon!!

I grabbed myself a coffee whilst I was waiting and people were arriving left, right and centre, some in groups, some solo walkers like me, runners too and supporting various charities.

Today I was walking in memory of my Nan, who we lost in August 22 to Dementia. This was my way of saying thank you to them for all their support that they gave us through Nans Dementia Journey, and a horrible journey that was. One of the cruelest illnesses you could have as you see your loved one slip away from you repeatedly until you say goodbye for the final time.

It was pitch black; the lights were shining bright as the floodlights lit up all the starting points. There were tables and chairs everywhere where people were starting to enroll and sit down and grab a drink ready before they ventured out.

5.50am and we got the call to go over for the warmup and I thought, this is it. This is really happening. I could feel the butterflies in my tummy thinking do I need a wee now before I get going, even though I have just been twice!!

The countdown commenced, 5, 4, 3, 2, 1 and we are off, walkers and runners off we go. Arundel here we come. The sun was just starting to come up. I had my hat on, and it was quite warm already, so I was a bit concerned about how hot it was going to get during the challenge. I was worrying already, nerves I assume but as I got into the swing of things I just started to enjoy the moment.

After crossing that start line, I first ventured out of Hove through a housing estate where I remember seeing so much litter. It was not the most pleasant start to a walk, but then we crossed over the main road over a bridge heading up on the downs towards Devil's Dyke.

It was thick fog this morning, so you didn't realise you were progressing up the hill, up through the various golf courses, of which I think we passed 3 different ones, and luckily, I was heading up the part I was most dreading Devils Dyke, and because of the adrenaline as well as the thick fog you just kept walking with the flow of the walkers.

About an hour into the adventure, I was just starting to make my way up onto the downs. Everywhere was marked with pink arrows, so you knew where you were going, and you just kept putting one foot in front the other to get you to the top of the hills. There were quite a few walkers on this first bit and a few runners too, that would let you know that they were behind you, so you could let them pass by.

The views were truly spectacular all over the downs, where you could see the bowls of the hills and lots of fields in the distance. Beautiful blue skies starting to come through and it was such an incredible feeling of being part of this epic event, something I never thought I would experience, certainly not so long after having my operation.

Around 7:15am as I was walking over the top of the various hills, you could look down into the bowls and the mist was sitting in them like a cauldron. Walking over the top of one of the hills before taking the descent down to the other side, to the left of me, close, there was a big bunch of cows roaming freely.

I remember walking next to the side of a few girls that were walking for Macmillan, and I started chatting to them. It was always good as a solo walker that whoever was on that walk, was always happy to talk to others and lift your spirits.

I said good morning to this cow and then I turned around and realised it was starting to follow me down the path. I moved a bit quickly to try and get across the cattle grids as this one was far too interested in me and as much as I love cows, I really did not want this one to get too close to me.

Still very misty and dewy, which was nice, because at this point, an hour and a half in, I was feeling the heat already and knew because of the weather in the prior weeks that we'd had, this certainly was going to be the hottest day of the year that we'd had so far.

I was expecting temperatures of 30 plus, which when you are walking a marathon, certainly for the first time, is not really what you want to be doing. But luckily the mist was keeping the temperatures down so far.

As soon as the sun broke out and the mist disappeared though, the heat started to really intensify. Walking up the next hill which just seemed to keep going on and on, with very loose flint under your feet, made it harder for walking I just continued heading up to Beeding Hill.

We were walking then along the riverside, and it was thick, thick fog, but it took us to our first stopping point, which was a very welcoming point when seeing that archway.

Not doing these before, I was not sure what to expect on the stop, so was refreshing to grab a cup of coffee and a nice, tasty danish pastry.

Then after a quick wee stop I started again, heading back over the South Downs, and I came across these pigs at the top of the hill, what seemed like hundreds and hundreds of pigs, hiding around their pig sties. The noise that they made, was unbelievable. They were everywhere and it was feeding time as the tractor driver came up and poured all the food into the troughs. You have never seen pigs run so fast to get their food. It was great to see them enroute though.

By 9:45am I had reached the 73 km point, so I had walked a total of 23 km at this point, as I had started at the 50km point. I thought taking on a 100km for my first ever challenge would be super crazy, I am not that mad.

In the distance you could see lots of sheep on the hills and the cyclists were out and lots of people venturing up towards yet another hill. This route was one of the harder hillier routes to start on, again not one of my brightest moments, I should have looked at the route in more detail before booking it up, but hey this is me again, diving into the unknown without my full research! I do like to challenge myself.

Everywhere you looked was just farmland, landscapes of fields and flint paths which seemed to continue on and on. Enjoying lots of wildlife, lots of cows, farmyard animals and by 10.15am I recognised the next part of the walk we were approaching.

This was Chanctonbury Ring, which I had luckily done a bit of training on that hill before, so I knew what to expect. However, instead of the route that I took last time I was here, we diverted left and ended up down in the Wiston Vineyard, which I did not even know was there. The grapes were looking amazing, but I did resist temptation.

The next stop we were heading for was Windlesham House School, and just after 11:15am, I had reached the 32 km sign (82km into the full challenge). I was actually a little emotional and I could tell that I was getting tired, and the heat was getting to me because at this point, I was starting to feel a little bit sick and shaky, and I got those tingling sensations in my nose that I always seem to get now when I'm walking and in need of drink or food or sugar. Maybe explains why I made a wrong turn earlier down by the vineyard and I did not realise until one of the others looked at me strangely. I did wonder why I had stopped seeing those pink arrows guiding us on the right route.

So pleased to see that second stop, and as I passed one of the walkers who had a trek master with them encouraging them to the next stop, I had realised she had been walking through the night and you could see she was absolutely shattered and in pain, and I felt such admiration for her as to what she was putting herself through to get to the next stop.

I have never been so happy to see a can of coke, and packet of Walkers salt and vinegar crisps. I did top that up with a banana and a wrap, which went down well before heading off at midday again, down to more parts of the walk that I had done previously before. This part of the route was becoming quite familiar.

In the distance I could see Amberley and crossing over a railway line over to our next check point, I really was starting to struggle now. I was hitting that 'Wall.' The heat was getting to me, my legs were becoming weak, and I did wonder at this point if I had just taken on too much.

As I embarked on my third stop of the day, I can remember picking up bags and bags of Haribo sour sweets which were great as I really needed the sugar fix and a big bottle of water because it was really, hot at this point of the day.

It was 2.15pm and I knew where this last stage was heading for because I had been here before. It was going to be almost 2 hours the way I was now walking before I got back to the finish line.

In a way, it was worse because I knew just how far I had to go, whereas on the previous parts of the walk, I did not know where I was going, so I was able to just keep putting one foot in front of the other and keep going.

Even though the heat was getting to me, I headed off, towards where the Riverside Cafe was in Amberley, walking alongside the waterside, which was refreshing to just hear that water, see the swans, and looking over the hills and the downs as to where we just walked from. I crossed over the lovely part of the bridge where you could see boats in the distance and all the hedgerows were full of blackberries.

Finally, at 3:51pm, I could see the finish line. I almost broke at this point as the emotions really started to hit me. Two volunteers were cheering me on saying *"your nearly there keep going you can do it."*

I could not believe it; I had come this far in getting that close towards the finish line. I was running so much on adrenaline; the tears were rolling down my face. I looked at the women that were standing there in their orange t-shirts and their red hats on, thinking I was so pleased and overjoyed with what I have done. I was also completely exhausted by the whole experience. It is an amazing, overwhelming sensation when you have achieved something like that.

I crossed that line with tears of happiness, knowing I had done this for my nan, that she had been with me on the way as every now and then when I was struggling a little robin would appear.

I picked up my medal and t-shirt with such pride and called Michael to tell him that I had done it, and he could venture down to collect me, luckily only 30 minutes away. I sat and collected my thoughts and emotions. After having a quick drink, I headed back to the car park in the town ready for Michael to pick me up.

That was hard though getting back up after sitting down for 10 minutes that is for sure and I struggled to put one foot in front of the other, I knew I should not have sat down.

When I got back, my feet and my legs were so swollen halfway up my legs, it was again like I had nettle rash, and boiling water put over my feet. I pulled off all the tape and the one thing I did not do in this walk was retape my feet at the halfway point. That is something I should have done but I came away with no blisters just very swollen legs.

But at that point, it was all a new experience to me, and I did not really know what to expect. I discovered after a nice cool bath that I had friction sores in places you never thought you would get, under your bra, your backside, inside your legs and on your arms, where things had obviously been rubbing and causing friction. However, it really was worth all the pain because I had achieved it. Something I never ever thought would be possible 18 months ago (or 9 months since walking again).

One thing that got me through when I had hit that struggling point at the third part of the challenge, that wall, was to remind myself of why I was doing the challenge in the first place.

This was for my nan and all those people that live with Dementia, and it was raising money for them and awareness too. I dug right down into my thoughts and had all those wonderful memories of my nan. I knew she had been flying by with me because I had seen a robin on many of the trees and roots as we were embarking on the challenge.

What also got me through was the amount of people that were messaging me, contacting me on Facebook, and sharing their words of inspiration and thoughts, along the way, it just helped so much.

You must dig so deeply into not just your physical strengths, but mental strength too. It really gave me a sense of personal achievement, taking on something and being able to complete it and I needed that. I needed to fulfil a challenge to know that what I did those 18 months ago, having that operation, really was the best thing that I could have done for myself. My life has transformed because of it.

October 23 – 'The Walk for the Waves'

Chichester to Selsey & Back - 42km (26 miles)

Fully recovered now after my Ultra Marathon Challenge, with a hint of itchy feet as I was missing the long walks, I decided that the time was right to get back into full training again. I was now preparing for my next challenge which I had booked a few days after crossing the finishing line in September, but this time it is not up those grueling hills but instead a flatter 50km Thames Path route during Easter 24.

Deciding to go further afield, I fancied something different and walking down to the sea felt like a good plan. So, I decided that today would be the day that I was going to drive to Chichester and then walk from Chichester to Selsey and back, like you do.

Looking at the App, it should take me between 8 and 9 hours which I had done previously on my challenge so knew I was now capable of walking this length of time.

Parking at Chichester, I walked down past the police station, heading towards the dual carriageway, and crossed over the bridge towards Hunston.

The sun was just making its way out through the clouds, and I knew it was going to be a lovely day, well I hoped the weather man was right as I did not fancy getting wet.

As I went over the top of the bridge across the A27, you could see the view of Chichester Free School where I had previously taken Harry to a karate tournament back when he was younger (and into those sorts of things). Now a teenager how it all changes!

Walking behind the back of the school, I approached the noise of diggers and cement mixers in the distance, with that building works smell in the air. Carrying on walking along the track, before I knew it, I had started to walk up by the Hunston Canal, which is one of my favourite places to go paddle boarding. The area was so still, the light of the sun was reflecting off the water, and such a calming and a tranquil place to be. The swans and ducks even came over to say hello which was a nice welcome.

As I made my way through the back of the houses, heading over the road and across a playing field, I walked up past the churchyard, after making a slight wrong turn, before heading on to some fields, full of sweetcorn, ready for harvest.

My next part of the route took me through yet another golf course, more to the side of it this time rather than back through the middle, which hopefully lessened the chance of me being hitting by a golf ball. Continuing through further fields, approaching a farm, my face lit up as yes, you guessed it, I approached a field full of cows, vast amounts of cows, as it looked to be a dairy farm.

Some of them had bells around them and some with tags which gave them that little shock when they got too close to the border line, something technical they do now which saves on the fencing!

Approaching a sign for the England Coastal Path, I made my way up to Sidlesham Quay, another wonderful place that I never knew existed. One of the reminders to myself why I love walking so much, is the voyage of discovery, it is so, so rewarding.

The tide was out, and I could see the mounds of sand dunes and lots of the teasels around the water's edge. I jumped as I came across a massive brown slow worm down by my feet. Panicking at first as I thought it was a snake, and I am not one who loves snakes!

As I made my way down to Church Norton and around the side of the water, I headed down to Selsey Beach, and arrived at Park Corpse, which was near Indiana's Sandpit and East Beach.

Continuing to walk on the pebbly part of the beach, which was not the easiest on my tired and hot feet, I discovered a long wooden slated walkway that was placed within the pebbles so you could safely get across saving more pain on your feet. I had forgotten just how hard it is to walk on these pebbles as your feet are forever sinking deep in the ground, and your ankles are twisting in all sorts of directions.

I was absolutely loving this walk, so different to my normal woodland views and breathing in the sea air absorbing the view out to sea was just what I needed. A place I could quite easily live that is for sure.

Off the pebbles I made my way up a track alongside the beach houses, where I discovered a very fascinating converted old train cabin which looked like it was a holiday retreat or a café. It was bright white, painted with a bright green door, and a great discovery.

By the side I stumbled upon a group of stunning burdock heads, golden and brown in the sun. The waves were not big today, but you could still hear the pebbles as they scraped across the sand, as they get dragged back out to sea.

Almost like a relaxing fizzing sound and I could sit here for hours just listening, and as tempting as it was, I knew there was an exceptionally long walk home.

Arriving at the beach just after midday after 3.5 hours walking, I was pleased with how far I had come but was ready for some lunch, so I headed into the town and stopped for a sandwich and drink before heading back on my way.

It was becoming very warm now and I was starting to get very tired legs, but I knew I could not give up, as I wanted to get back before 4pm. I knew although it had only taken me 3.5 hours to get to this point, it was likely to take me over four on the way back as I was bound to be slower.

As I headed back, making my way past Church Norton, I was in Sidlesham Quay before I knew it, but this time the tide was coming in, so it looked so different than I had seen it this morning.

I then seemed to arrive, not sure how on a slightly different route back, which took me across a field where I ended up at the back of someone's garden. I crossed a little stream where I could see a gate to get me on the main road where I needed to be.

I remember this man saying, *'oi you, you can't walk down here, it's not a public footpath this is my garden."* I said, "I'm so, so sorry, I think I had misread my app, I am walking back from Selsey, and I couldn't work out where I was going, my brains not functioning properly." He laughed, and kindly let me through his gate to get back on to the main road so I could venture back on track.

Making my way on the right path now next I went through the farmlands, before heading onto the golf course. I came across a collection of old machinery; there was an ancient old bulldozer, a crane, an old fire engine and a JCB, all rusting away, but what a stunning collection of old machinery to have. I knew Michael would be impressed and jealous too!!

Approaching Mill Pond Halt, I came to a sign put up by Sidlesham Parish Council telling me about the walkway which was remarkably interesting. I discovered I was walking the 'Old Selsey Tramway,' which is a walking trail tracing the route of the hundreds of Manhood and Selsey tramways from 1897 to 1935. The total length between Chichester and Selsey was 11.8 miles, and you can walk it in short sections and return by bus.

Enroute today I walked with lovely butterflies, and one followed me on the way back through the fields. It was a beautiful bright orange butterfly with unique markings like the stunning red and elegant Admiral butterflies.

The detail on the sides of her wings reminded me of an Asian butterfly, the way it was jaggedly cut around its wings with such precision.

This walk was a lot further than I had planned in my head today and at times I questioned my route as I struggled with the heat. Although you plan a route and you see it on a map, when you are walking it, at times you do think that you made the wrong decision with the route.

However, my reassurance on this route was that if I needed it, there were plenty of bus stops on the way back. I told myself if I felt that the walk was simply getting too much, I would jump on the bus back to the beginning. Knowing I didn't want to be defeated though, I just took it steadily and I thought if I could mentally get to the next bus stop, I would finally get myself back and it worked.

My feet were ridiculously hot and swollen from this walk and as much as I enjoyed the walk, on the way back I was really struggling as I had walked for just over 8 hours in the heat and walked 42 km.

I would do this walk again and although it was tough at times, more so on the way back it was a very enjoyable one and has become my 'Walk of The Waves.'

I took a risk today, taking on yet another adventure, into the unknown pushing myself but it paid off as I experienced unfamiliar places and achieved something I did not think I could do.

Today also being by the sea gave me that freedom of thought that I needed to process Grandad becoming a permanent resident at Rotherlea. Due to him being more unstable, suffering more with fragility and dementia, he simply was not able to cope at home anymore. It was extremely hard knowing that he would never go back to his home in Hampers Green.

During the last few months since he first stayed at Rotherlea, he had made an enormous impact on the staff as they were all starting to get to know him, his funny ways, and sense of humour.

But now I believe he has finally settled and now called this his home, there has even been times where he was thinking he was back in Hampers Green cooking his dinner, so in his mind he was home which was reassuring.

Dealing with the Dementia, a second time around I found extremely hard, and so different to that of nans. A combination of the dementia alongside his Charles Bonnett Syndrome meant we were all on a very emotional rollercoaster, having such good days and then such bad days.

Each day that arrived, you never knew how grandad was going to be. This was so hard emotionally, but every now and then I would see my old grandad, only for a few moments and I knew he was still there, inside, just fronted with a confused body.

It was also so nice to know that the carers had such fun looking after grandad and he was happy in his surroundings, which gave me comfort that grandad was in the right place. Today I realised this by having this needed time and space in nature which has given me healing and help. Walking has certainly been so helpful when trying to sort things out in your mind.

November 23 – 'My Cow Selfie Walk'

Bepton, Midhurst Brickworks & West Lavington 14km (9 miles)

Well, I certainly regretted not having my gaiters on this morning, why I did not put them on I do not know, rushing out early when you are still half asleep has something to do with it.

Heading out at 6.30am, this route is a regular route I often do now, which takes me over Midhurst Common, through to Bepton, venturing back across to Midhurst Brickworks and then heading across up to West Lavington, through Midhurst and back home. About a 14km route taking about 3 hours, and its lovely doing it first thing watching the sun come up as it invigorates you, starting your day in a positive way.

As I start off my route this morning heading over Midhurst Common, I can hear a lot of black crows in the top of the pine trees, squawking and squabbling and pigeons too. I think, whatever walk you go on, you are forever seeing pigeons, they seem to be one of those birds that are everywhere.

Making my way over the common which is still extremely wet, I walk into Bepton, which is a familiar starting point for me, because it can take me on many routes.

Whether I am heading from here to Chichester, or whether I am walking up Cocking Hill and across through to Harting, it is always my chosen starting point. Mainly because I stop off at The Country Inn and get a fantastic cup of coffee and sometimes my fuel for a morning's walk, which can often be a chocolate chip cookie. Not the healthiest I know.

Samo and I start to approach the main road, and you can hear all the old classic cars and sports cars, as they are revving their engines, going down to Goodwood being the first Sunday of the month. My son always likes me to take photographs for him so he can see what cars are heading down.

A little Jenny Wren pops out of the hedge in front of me, such a pretty, dainty little bird, but my ultimate favourite is the Nuthatch, which I have only seen once on this route, in one of the trees, back up towards the Country Inn.

Jenny Wrens are truly magical little birds with their tall tails sticking up in the air, they are just like little balls of joy and my son Harry loves these, definitely one of his favourites.

Blackbirds are hovering in the overgrowth and there are an abundance of stinging nettles thriving in this weather. The fog's not broken completely but is starting to lift and often that is a sign of a good day, so I am told.

As I walk past the pond, I cannot see the anglers you often see fishing today, or the heron that stands on guard of his fish, but just three little ducks swimming across in a line, one by one.

Hearing the motorbikes in the distance zooming through Midhurst, it is often the sound you would hear on a Sunday morning walk. As I walk along, looking up at the trees and the sky I can just hear the echo of a woodpecker in the oak trees in front of me, such an amazing sound, just like when you hear the cuckoo for the very first time.

The fog is becoming much thicker again, and I cannot see much in front of me, but I can still hear the pheasants in the fields, and I always know if they are close as Samo can sense them too and his ears prick up.

I just get a glimpse of the cows up in the distance as we get closer through to the farm, and they are just all standing there now, looking at me, watching me go by, eyes peeled. No doubt thinking, there is that crazy woman again who keeps stopping and taking selfies.

Looking deeper at what is in front of me, I capture on the fence line, the barbed wire, where the spiders have tried to get across the top of the spikes leaving wonderful, elegant spider webs in their tracks.

You can just see them glistening in the sun. Further along I see three beautiful stinging nettles with the white flowers starting to grow from inside, at the top one of the fence posts. It really is amazing to see and makes me wonder how things find places to grow.

At this point, we are just approaching three miles into the walk and the robin has just appeared out of the hedge way in front of me. We continue to walk up past the Midhurst Brickworks and continue till we walk under the old railway bridge. There is a number dotted around this area, and you can walk, I believe, from Midhurst to Chichester, following the old railway bridges.

I am feeling the chill now in my fingers, the Raynaud's creeping in again and maybe it was a day that I should have brought my gloves, but I was hoping that the sun was going to come out and warm up quickly.

As we come up to the main road, the tractors whizz past and it looks like the mole's been active in places along people's lawns this morning too. 3.5 miles in, we are heading back down over the main road where we cross over to West Lavington as we then head up past the Royal Oak Pub.

The sun is getting higher in the sky and becoming quite bright, but still patchy fog in places, so you still cannot see much in front of you. As we get further up after the little humpback bridge, there is a field often full of deer freely roaming but as we approach it, I cannot see them, it is just purely the peaceful sounds again of the wind through the trees and the birds chirping.

The cars become more distant, and I come across three beautiful white horses in the field to the right of me, grazing with their warm coats on.

The fog has finally lifted, and the sun is out. Such a special time of the day for me and it certainly rejuvenates you and uplifts you ready for the day ahead.

This route through West Lavington always brings back special memories for me. When I had had my first son, Jack, at the time living in West Lavington, I would often stroll this route with the pushchair trying to get him off to sleep.

That was just over some 20 years ago now, but how the route is unchanged. It is always nice reliving those moments and that is what I find often with the walks now, something you see takes you back to a place from years ago.

You will always remember something of your walks and that has enabled me to put together this book for you today, as I look through the photographs I took, the routes I took, I was able to relive all those moments, those feelings and be back there in an instance. Walking definitely enables me to create new memories as well as discovering new paths and places.

Carrying on up my route today and noticing on many other routes previously that I have walked, is just how many of the trees are now starting to fall or be uprooted. Massive trees, to do with all this damp weather we are having, they are just rotting at the bottom and falling over, crashing through fences, and causing destruction. Yet it is amazing how they continue to grow.

They do not die off, they just uplift and although uprooted, they still hang in there, creating new life but in a different direction. It amazes me how nature finds a way of growing in the most unexpected places. As I approach 4.5 miles, I have been walking for just under 2 hours, and the robin has come again to say hello in front of me on the path. She made sure I saw her before she bounced away, and that is my nan still walking beside me when I am out.

The dog's nose is working on overdrive pulling my arm as he keeps stopping trying to smell all those interesting smells. They say that's how dogs read the daily newspaper, isn't it?

They use their nose as a form of seeing what has been going on. Whereas we choose to flick on Facebook and watch the news to catch up.

Two little rabbits in the distance bouncing around obviously just heard me as they shot across the dewy field. Always lovely to see the wildlife in the morning.

It really does make a walk special when you are constantly seeing different wildlife, along with hearing them on your way. You can really absorb the sounds, the air, the smell, the colours, and the creations that nature gives us to look at.

Some of these trees have been here for hundreds of years and you just wonder at, that point in time, who were these people that would have planted these trees, what else were they doing in their day? Who was walking down this road back then? Where were they walking?

As I walked past my old house, to me, it has not changed. It still looks the same and holds those special memories. We continue walking down to the bridge before hitting the back entrance to Cowdray House, and we do a left here at the junction to take you back up into Midhurst. In three miles if you headed to the right, you would reach Selham but today we are taking a left through St Johns Walk back to our starting point.

On the corner as we turn up to St Johns Walk there is a house that always gives me the jibes. It is one of those houses that looks haunted, but I am sure it is not, it just reminds me about a house in Petworth called Somerset Lodge, which was always one of the houses of my childhood I was always worried about walking past.

The suns behind me now and it is quite a pleasant feeling on my back as it starts to warm up and the skies are starting to get bluer. The fog has completely lifted, and you can see the various lines where the aeroplane streams have been in the sky. People are starting to get up and about as it is just after 8:30am and we have runners and walkers zooming past us now on this beautiful morning.

It is quite funny looking up above, you see two geese flying so hard, racing each other and they look like their wings are going to fall off. I wonder what goes through their minds when they are flying? Are they as competitive as us humans?

As we are approaching the Old Cowdray Dairy, which they are currently renovating, I am six miles in, and the path now has dried out which is such a joy as this is another one that can get very muddy when we have had a lot of rain. I have just walked over 2 hours and now we are going to be heading back up towards Bepton, heading through the duck pond and past the fire station to go back through Midhurst Common to head home.

By the time we get back, it will be just over nine miles and it is a regular route I will continue to do. Nice and flat, with lots of wildlife to see and a circular route with a coffee stop, or two on the way. If you ever get a chance to do this one and have a few spare hours, it is one that you will see lots of wildlife and simply enjoy being out in nature.

November 23 – 'Walking 300 miles for Prostate Cancer Research'

November 23 was definitely the month for rain and not the ideal month to take on another fundraising challenge!! This time, I had chosen to join the 'Walk 60 Miles in November for Prostate Cancer Research'. Knowing that 60 miles in a month, is often what I was now walking during the week, I thought I would up the goal and aim for 240 miles which worked out approx. 8 miles a day, and at the time seamed doable.

Venturing off on the first few days in the rain, it was much harder and slower walking. I was forever dodging the muddy puddles, the streams and rivers that were developing around the woods had become at times impassable. I carried on though, heading out early in the morning often at sunrise, waterproofs on, coming back with a very wet and smelly dog, and plenty of dirty wet clothes around with the evidence I had been out yet again across the countryside.

At first this was a refreshing goal to aim for, but as the days went on, and the rain kept coming, it was getting harder and harder to achieve. My walks took me around Cowdray, Bepton, Midhurst Common and the local woods but soon the places I found I could walk became limited due to the walking conditions. The normal pathways were flooded and often the side of the walks became dangerous to walk. November the rain just kept coming, but I still ventured out, and as hard as it was in torrential rain and bitterly cold winds. There were times that I really questioned myself as to why I had taken on another challenge so soon. But at the back of my mind, I knew friends that had passed from Prostate Cancer, and right now friends and colleagues going through Cancer treatment, and I was doing this for them. Also, my own men including my two sons, my dad and my partner, thinking one day it could be them this is happening too, and knowing that I did a little to help with the fundraising for research was a big enough reason to keep me going through these harder walks.

Raising money for charity, gave me that boost I needed on those wet, miserable days when I was soaked through to the bone, squelching in my walking boots, as some puddles where just too much to handle. At least the one benefit I found with the waterproof socks, is when you do get water inside them, you end up having a foot spa with warm water in your socks on the way home! Posting daily updates on my social media, I also had such great support and messages from friends and family that kept me going in these horrible walking conditions.

But my feet did pay the price over the time in walking in the rain, but luckily, I discovered 'Trench Cream' which helped, as the waterproof socks didn't at this point cope with these ridiculous weather conditions.

However, some of the days were dry days, and although cold which never helped with the Raynaud's, it was such a pleasant feel on your face as the sun warmed you up and put a smile on your face. I had almost forgotten what a dry path looked like.

Within my first five days I knocked up 45 miles, combining walking at sunrise and sunset, which was really magical capturing both parts of the day. Day 8 was probably the wettest of all the days, tackling an 8-mile route doing The Badger Walk. No where seemed to be safe to walk, even the roadways where full of deep puddles, so this was certainly the hardest month of the year to take on this challenge.

Day 11 though, the sun was shining bright, seeing the deer in the foggy distance, the baby cows in the cowshed and the robin continuing to be beside me as I walked on one of my local routes. Walking past Easebourne church on Day 12, Remembrance Sunday there were beautiful red cast poppies everywhere remembering those that had fallen, and remembering that without those that gave their lives, we wouldn't be experiencing the countryside like we do now.

By Day 27, the shin splints were starting to reemerge, and it was looking like I needed a revisit back to the physio for work on my hips and legs. I had probably overwalked again by setting myself this challenge.
Not wanting to be defeated I carried on and I had reached my goal. Asking my followers whether they

thought I should stop for a rest or carry on and aim for 300, a nice round number to finish of the month, people mentioned that I would miss it if I stopped, and they were probably right.

Even being out in the rain, which was horrible at times, you still found enjoyment, looking at all the beautiful views, the animals, discovering heart shaped leaves on the floor, the crisp frosty leaves, and the crunch of the frost underneath your feet as you ventured across a field. There was always a positive you could find on your route, and with the beautiful sunrises that I often saw every day in November, it became the perfect reason to get out early.

Wearing out my walking boots too, in such awful conditions they certainly needed replacing by the end of November, as the mud and water didn't help, as well as now walking over 1000 miles this year in them. I knew I would need to wear in new walking boots for my next challenge as I certainly had learnt on all my walks so far, you have to walk in comfortable boots otherwise you pay the price.

I achieved the 300 miles and thought time for a break now, slow down, give yourself a rest for a few weeks and maybe then in the New Year start training for April 24 Easter 50km Challenge that I had signed up to raise money for Macmillan Cancer.

December 23 - 'Back to Childhood Memories Walk'

Petworth Park Circular 12km (7 miles)

Middle of December, and a chilly winters day, I decided that I would take a route down memory lane, walking around the longer circular route of Petworth Park, a 700-acre Deer Park.

The sun was trying to find its way through the clouds, and it was going to be a nice dry day, which made a change as at this point as I had been fed up with walking in rain, puddles, and thick mud. Parking up at Rotherlea Nursing Home, as I popped in to see grandad before I went, I headed up to the side entrance of the park by the Cricket Club on the Tillington Road.

Looking over to the Upper Pond, I ventured over to the side of the Petworth House and The Tijou Gate (the deer park entrance) before heading down over the hills towards the kennels.

This reminded me of those times I would choose this route when walking with our old dog Bodie, who is remarkably like our dog Samo now, just reverse in his colourings, but with all the same funny ways and kind nature.

The skies where so blue as I approached the top of the hill, and it was starting to become a really settled day. The grass was bright green on the banks and covered in places with the brown copper leaves that had fallen from the trees, making them look bare but it made the deer much easier to spot.

There were so many deer in the park today, everywhere you looked you could see them in the distance, walking across the path in lines where others were huddled under the trees in groups, all with their unique markings, and most of them looking incredibly young.

They were almost three shades of brown with the darkest at the top, toning down to a very pale underneath. Some had the little white dots on their back whereas others had the chestnut brown.

I ventured down to the Lower Lake where when we were kids we would sit on the edge of the pond, dangling our feet down in the corner of the pond, a part where your feet did not get wet and watch for the fish and the pond skaters to swim across.

Keeping to the right-hand side around by the wall I would venture up towards the top car park and in the distance, I could see several large stags with their bold and brave antlers, and as they turned away, they had white and black marked heart shaped backsides.

I walked around the wall of the park, walking pass the tower and approaching a small unique black cast iron monument, I was intrigued to know what this was and have yet to discover, a memorial of some type.

Continuing on heading over to the top of Monument Hill I stood and captured the sun going behind the clouds and as I took a photo of this special moment, I had a green orb in the picture, so I knew someone was close with me on my walk, maybe my nan today as she lived the other side of the park too.

The clouds were settling in, and the sun had gone, as I walked through muddy, slippery leaves over to some amazing trees. Some that have been there for hundreds of years, and still stand tall and proud, whilst others had fallen in the storms including the Great Storm of October 1987.

There was one spectacular tree that had gone over with the force of the wind, and it looked like finger roots coming out of the ground, just like a big hand that stretched out.

I believe from the National Trust Website that it states that *"several of the trees at Petworth Park are ancient trees including three ancient oak trees, one of which was a sapling during the Norman conquest of 1066. There is a 'Beelzebub' oak which dates back to 1779, Sweet Chestnuts up to 600 years old of which some are gnarled and twisted from lightning strikes and a hollow common lime tree which is at least 500 years old"*. I remember as kids, Claire and I used to hide in when we were venturing into the park.

Walking back down one of the hills which was exceedingly difficult as it was very slippery due to the rain and the wet muddy leaves, I came across two beautiful stags, heads down eating the grass side by side. One was a rich deep dark velvet brown, and the other was a beige and white spotted one, so delicate.

As I made my way down the hills, they could hear me with the leaves rustling under my footsteps and their heads shot up and they started to move away, then there were others that followed in a line, six in total I counted. Some had fully grown antlers whilst others you could see were only slightly formed, or damaged as they were shorter.

The sun kept coming out and going in behind the clouds as I approached the Lower Lake, which I wanted to walk all the way around, enjoying those childhood memories I had of the lake.

Stopping at the Boat House which always holds memories of when my uncles were rebuilding that part many years ago, I remember being so happy and content. Happy with life, even with its difficult moments that we were having with grandad at the time.

I remember taking a selfie, having rosy, red cheeks, and was feeling alive and happy and so excited to go back to grandad to tell him I had walked around the whole of the park, something that always seemed boring and impossible when I was a child, how things have changed. This is now such a pleasurable place to walk, and I was so lucky to have this as a place to visit daily when I was a child.

Walking around the pond I looked over to see the wonderful Dog Monument (Dog of Alcibiades), sat in the middle of the pond with the ducks swimming around in their dozens making a racket like they do. Heading around the whole of the pond I then made my way back to the nursing home to see grandad yet again.

The route in total was about 12km, just over seven miles and a nice, relaxed route with a few difficulties on the various hills. Hard in places where the mud and leaves had made slippery walkways but a perfect route bringing back those precious memories of my days growing up.

Heading back, I explained the route to grandad that I had taken, as he was always interested in where I had been and what I had planned. Although his dementia had kicked in and he had his good and bad days, he was always still sharp as a button and knew where I was walking. He knew I was training hard for my next challenge in April 24, and it was always such a pleasure talking him through my discoveries and new routes.

Looking back 1 year ago when I was planning to achieve five miles, I am so much fitter and stronger than I ever thought I would be and would have to pinch myself sometimes as to how far I have come.

I am proud of myself for what I have achieved and although it has not all been plain sailing, I think once you have your heart set into something so much, you do not actually realise how far you have come in such a brief time.

This today was a nice gentle walk and if you have a spare 3 hours and you want the magnificent views of seeing the deer and the ponds and just being out somewhere in a circular enclosed route, then it is certainly one that you would enjoy.

Boxing Day 23 to 31st March 24

Start of the 800-mile Arctic Virtual Challenge

Knowing, I had my next Ultra Marathon Challenge, 50km April 6th, 2024, I needed to keep up my training plan which was harder as the weather was always wet, dark and gloomy. Everywhere was saturated and it was so hard to find the get up and go to get out early mornings, where I would rather be stuck in bed.

Things were getting harder with grandad, and I knew I had to keep walking for my own mental health as it really helped me in dealing with what was going on. But I just struggled finding that push I needed so looking at the Ultra Challenge Events a New Virtual Challenge had been set which gave you the option of doing 100, 200, 400 or 800 miles between Boxing Day 23 and March 31st, 2024.

Working that out daily and how many days I had to complete I thought what a perfect training schedule that would be and signed up ready for the start. Throughout this time, I ventured out daily doing eight miles a day and some days more making sure I had the mileage completed and I have chosen my favourite walks for you that I ventured out on during this wet, miserable time. Thank God for my Sealskinz Waterproof Socks!!

December 23 – 'The Butterfly Walk'

The Durleighmarsh Circular throughout the year - 8km (5 miles)

One route that was only a few miles away from home, and certainly has become one of my regular routes when I've got a couple of hours to spare, is driving over to Petersfield and walking the Petersfield to Durleighmarsh circular route. This is a route I have ventured in the different seasons too, seeing so many wonderful aspects of nature.

Parking at the Heath in Petersfield, I would make my way through the town heading out to the main A272, Midhurst to Petworth Road, cutting across the back of the fields, which takes you up through the lines of fruit trees after the 'bent tree', through some wooded areas, where you approach the back of the fields of Durleighmarsh Farm, often stopping at the Tea barn for refreshments halfway round.

To continue the route, you would head across the main road, over the fields again, past the large oak tree in the centre of the field and head back through to the Petersfield Heath finishing where you first started.

A perfect lovely circular route, with a few small inclines, about 2.5 hours long and 8km. Often, I would do this route in reverse to experience what the views had to offer when looking at it from a different direction.

Spring - March 23 is when I first ventured on this walk, a bright sunny day, after various diversions I am ending up walking 11km in just under 3 hours. At this time of year, I enjoyed walking through the bluebell foliage as you approached the wooded section as they were waiting for their blooms, which you knew would be spectacular later on in the year. In the distance as you walked to its highest point over the fields. you looked over beautiful green fields, full of rich grass and the cloudy skies slowly covering the sky, hiding the sun on its way.

Walking back over to the heath, you came across bright yellow gorse bushes and as I approached the bridge with the water gushing below, I made my way up to a discovery of cows in the field before heading back onto the Petersfield Heath.

The highlight at this time was seeing the bright yellow daffodils out in full bloom, and even though the pathways which were still full of brown fallen leaves and wet muddy tracks, the route was still enjoyable, even with a muddy dog who had decided to walk his way through the muddy fields and paths.

Not so pleasant in the car on the way home though, the windows certainly needed opening as the smell was a little too much for the nose.

Spring - April 23 I repeated the walk but in reverse, always something I do now to see nature from a different view. It was another bright blue day, and today I came across the carpets of blue and white bells where previously it was just the green foliage. The sky was clear and bright with no clouds to block the sun, the fields where lusciously bright green and so where the trees.

I came across a digger in a field just by the fruit trees which looked like it was levelling out the rough ground after we had had so much torrential rain. A beautiful Admiral butterfly landed in front of me, and what a stunning sight that was. The pink nettles where shining in the sun and Samo and I were loving getting out in the sunshine after we had so much rain recently.

You had glimpses of the wood sorrel as we walked through the woods, and in the distance, they were laying the plastic on the fields at the back of Durleighmarsh Farm to protect the crops from the elements. Looking up the hedgerows were full of berries and yellow gorse; Spring was definitely here and such a perfect place to see such vibrant colours as you made your way around the route.

Summer - June 23 was my third visit and today really was the hottest day I had walked this route. Having the sun shining seemed to make me pick up my speed as today I managed it in just over 2 hours, as the paths were drier and easier to walk on. There is nothing like a wet muddy field to slow you down.

Walking through the fields, the wheat was so high, you could not see much in the distance and would not until it had ripened ready for the combines and the tractors to harvest it later on in the year. It was definitely hot weather today which made a change from marching out in your waterproofs in the pouring rain!

The views where spectacular and today I stopped at the Tea Barn enjoying a Passion Fruit Sorbet and Coke to cool me down. Poppies and daisies were popping out in the fields and the grasses where super high, the ferns so tall and Samo would often disappear into them, sniffing his way around to see what he could find.

Bright Pink Foxgloves where out in full bloom and coming across the small river before you headed back into the town the water glistened, such a perfect day.

During this walk I was swarmed with different butterflies. I remember calling it the 'Butterfly Walk,' because every species of butterfly, I could see I saw today. Black and white ones, yellow ones, the red ones, the orange ones, white and blue ones, they were all flying around me, I was the butterfly whisperer!

Winter - Mid December 23 –Today I walked for over 2.5 hours in torrential rain. I was getting soaked right through, even though I had my waterproofs on, it was that heavy I was not the happiest of bunnies that is for sure.

Luckily Samo did not seem to mind though, he never worried what the weather was doing as long as he was venturing out in the countryside. Coming across some marshy boggy land as I had walked through one of the fields, I came across the woodland path which was full of mud and slippery slopes.

It was always so hard walking in the mud as you had to straddle the paths to try and avoid the large deep holes or the rivers of water that would make their way down.

Everywhere you walked it was mud, glorious mud and not much to see in the way of wildlife and flowers, just the holly bushes and sad looking trees as they had lost their leaves.

Funnily enough I cannot remember seeing a sole on this walk, probably as they were not crazy like me to walk in these conditions, but I always tried to venture out whatever the weather was doing to make the most of these opportunities and get out the door.

Winter - January 24, another wet walk, but not as wet as the time I walked this before back in December. Today I could see peaking underneath the fallen wet leaves, a large number of white snowdrops looking for that light as they poked their little heads through.

I was covered up with my waterproofs that were working today and my big woolly hat as it was cold as well as wet, but underneath I was cozy and warm, well at least for now I was dry.

After a while it warmed up, the rain stopped, and the sun came out. With my temperature issues setting in once again, I just had to take my coat off before I overheated, but no doubt it will be back on in the next 10 minutes as I would be cold again.

The fields where saturated and the muddy fields made it so hard for walking, but I was so pleased the sun was out as at least I started to dry out.

As I came towards the end straight of the walk the clouds were filling in and, in the distance, I could see my favourite Oak Tree that I loved looking at on the walk.

Walking through over to the rivers side, it became harder to walk and my feet were sliding everywhere, at this point the waterproof socks were starting to fail me as the water in places had gone over my boots and into the top of my socks, so today it was certainly a 'Coat On, Coat off, Wet Feet' kind of a day! My walking boots were caked in mud and before getting in the car I had to change them before covering the car in mud.

Always enjoy taking Samo on this route because it was a nice short route that he enjoyed too, but it was never nice on the journey home when it had been raining and the car became full of wet doggy smells.

This walk will always be one of my favourite walks as it is flat, relaxing, and close by. If you ever have the pleasure to discover this route, then you can choose your starting point either at the Durleighmarsh Farm or Petersfield Heath and make your way round. The bonus point about having a Circular Route rather than a point to point, you can pick your starting point that suits you.

January 24 - 'The Miniature Snail Walk!'

Bepton - Easebourne - Older Hill – Woolbeding Common - 22 km (14 miles)

It was one of those days that I listened in bed to the rain pounding and hitting the window, thinking just another ten more minutes before I decide it might calm down. That was going on from 5:30am and then 10 minutes later I thought, no, come on, you can do this, stop being so lazy. Just because it is raining, it is not an excuse to not get out there and not put your walking boots on.

So, I prepped all up, making sure I had my waterproofs on, Sealskinz hat, my waterproof socks, and my gaiters to try and minimise how wet I would get. Then off we went (Samo and I) venturing into the dark wet countryside. Luckily for me, Samo does not mind the rain, I think he would walk with me wherever I went as long as he could have a sniff and a run on the way.

Today I decided we are going to tackle a 13 – 14 mile route, which took us firstly to Bepton, our regular coffee stop to get us going.

Off then back down to Cowdray Ruins, across to Easebourne, then up Easebourne Street until we get to the top towards Bexley Hill. We would then take a left down past Verdley Farm, across the main road, over to Kings Drive, and up to Older Hill where we would then head back down through the woods at Woolbeding Common, down to Eastshaw Lane. This would take us back home, unless we extended the route for another coffee but that all depends on how wet we get!! So that was the planned route and I hoped to get back within 4 – 5 hours.

I know when you look out the window and see all the drizzle, wind, and rain, when its pounding and blowing a gale, but if you have the right attire, then actually it is nice walking in the rain. I love just listening to the raindrops hitting the leaves, and puddles on the pavement beside you making bubbles as it hits the ground.

You just need to watch where you are footed because obviously paths can turn muddy really quickly and become very slippery, but walking in the rain is something I actually love doing and that is a good job too because we've had a lot of rain to walk through over the last few months.

As we walked a lot of offroad, the paths were often thick mud and slop, and this route was a combination of both roads and woods so it would be an interesting walk today. I would often tell myself it is all good training for my next event when you are walking in these conditions, because on the day you just never know what the weather is going to be. It is never always going to be the perfect walking conditions. Within the first 10 minutes we are already tackling quite deep puddles as we head down to Bepton. Samo is black underneath and who knows what colour he will by the time we have finished.

One thing that does make walking a lot easier for me these days is when I converted from glasses to contact lenses, because now I do not get steamed up whenever it rains. It is so much nicer to see where you are going too! This came about after doing my first Ultra Marathon due to the extreme heat, and the sweat on my face, my glasses kept sliding down my nose and I was forever picking them up and putting them back on.

This became extremely frustrating, so I thought I would invest in testing contact lenses again, which I had worn many, many years ago. Well certainly for walking it has made everything so much easier. You have not got to worry about losing your glasses in the woods as well as constantly keep wiping them to see where you are heading.

Today all the green trees have a real glisten to them, and they shine with such beauty and light. What I do love watching is the little rain droplets that accumulate on the edge of the leaves, seeing the formations as they build until they cannot cope anymore, and they drop off the side.

If you are very clever with your camera, you can capture that dropping sensation, but I have never yet managed to picture that moment. The pitter patter on your cap that you can hear is what I love. Luckily, this morning's it is not as heavy as what I thought it was going to be. I still have my head torch on as it is still dark, but we can still get a beautiful view of what is going on including the splashes as the raindrops hit the puddles makes big bubbles along the side of the road.

What you do not want now is someone to drive past you on the side of the road and cover you with these deep puddles, because that is never a pleasant experience and luckily has not happened to me too many times.

Certainly, so peaceful this morning as there are not any people as crazy as me to get out at this time of the morning, they are all sensible and tucked up in bed. But there is something special about being out at this time, seeing the sunrise and watching the day unfold, I love it and have been so lucky to capture some beautiful photos of these moments.

Above I see two ducks flapping hard again. They are the two competitive racers that I have seen before, training for a marathon too. It is amazing how their wings do not fall off!

Today I am naming this walk the 'Snail Walk.' The enjoyment you get out watching these tiny little snails walk across walls as we head down into Bepton by the houses. There seem to be an abundance of them today and must be to do with the damp weather. Something I cannot remember seeing so many of this early on in the day. To me that is why being out in nature is so special and I am finding I am so more observant now than I ever used to be. I am always looking out for those smaller things that just brighten my day.

Capturing these encounters of nature is so special and it is just something you can never experience when you are driving your car. You have to actually get out there and walk places, and not even far, to see these wonderful pleasures. Seeing those intricate details like the moss that is growing on the wall and how the little furs and the little stems just get into those minute little cracks is so interesting. Try it.

As you start to look deeper at things around you, you start noticing things like the cracks in the wall too, where trees have started to grow through them and find their way to the light.

That is always something mesmerising about these creations, and you wonder just how do they get there? How is that still growing? It is amazing how you see things grow in places you would never expect.

So, within 40 minutes, my dear robin has made its presence known and past next to me on the roadway as Samo and I are both walking down the pathway alongside the road heading towards Midhurst.

My legs and calves feel a bit heavier today, so I have got to listen to my body and keep an eye on them. They are just giving me those little warning signs, but hopefully it is just that they have not woken up yet, but as I learnt the hard way before I am being more in tune with my body now.

In the beginning, when walking was new to me, all I was interested in was increasing my mileage and my new repeated word in my head was mileage, mileage, mileage. I really did push myself because I thought my body could cope with the adjustments as my head was telling me it was ok; however, I have learnt that you really need to do it carefully.

A maximum of 10% increase on your mileage each week is recommended not the 70% increase jumps that I did back in the beginning where I ended up doing damage and instead of moving forward you take five steps back. Thankfully, I have always had a fantastic physio to support me with my walking, Bill at Perfect Motion Physio helped me when I had over walked!! I knew that I had overdone it when I started getting shin splits, as well as having issues and pains with my hips. They were causing me grief today, and walking was becoming unpleasant, but as I did not want to give up, I kept pushing myself forward, not something I should be doing. I needed to give my body the time to recover.

Having people around you, like the physios and specialists that you trust when it comes to your health, who can guide you into the right ways of doing things, especially when it is all new, I found out was essential. Approaching the gates to the entrance of a garden as I am heading into Midhurst, the robin is sitting there watching me, making sure I am going in the right direction. There is always something warming and special knowing the robin's close by.

Looking down on the floor, everywhere you look, you see the snails trying to climb up everything! I have just seen a few tiny little snails trying to get from one stinging nettle leaf to another. How do they hold on to those big blades of grass? How does the weight of a snail hold onto a very minute thin stick?

Approaching Cowdray early in the morning, is another place I've walked in all conditions, whether it be sun, frost, snow, ice, wind and torrential rain, the views as you capture the sun coming up over the ruins or the polo fields can be spectacular, but you have to be quick as one minute it is there and the next it is gone.

As we make our way pass the railings looking over to the Round House, the light captures the spider's webs as it is just turning to daylight. Again, like the snails something you do not normally pay any attention to, but the spider webs become remarkably interesting.
You look at all their creations and how unique each of them is. How do some spiders get from one side of the railings to the other across the road? It is just magical. Absolutely magical.

You can see the polo fields in the distance and one of my favourite trees on this route is approaching, in fact one I have made a canvas at home as I captured the beautiful sunrise behind it. We head up towards the sand piles, which is always a favourite place for Samo. He really loves this part, and he transforms into a teenager again that just literally fills him with life and he goes crazy.

I can feel his energy as he just looks at me, to check it is okay to go mad for another five minutes before we head off on our route. We have such a true bond, and he has been such an amazing part of my journey, walking with me as we are enjoying unfamiliar places together. I love the way, when we get to a path or junction, he always looks at me as if to say, "well, are we going this way today or that way"? Think he gets confused as to which path we are taking, as we often change our routes to making it more interesting.

The fog's mist is just starting to lift in the distance, right over the golf course, and you can start to see the day brightening. It is still light rain, but you can cope with this sort of rain. It is when its torrential rain it becomes harder to walk in. There are many times that I have gone out and got absolutely soaked through to the bone and cannot wait to get back home for a hot shower and into some fresh clean clothes.

However, there is actually something quite refreshing about the cool rain when you are hot and probably by the feel of me, red faced like a tomato and I have only walked four miles so far too. I have got about another 8 or 10 to go yet, so who knows what I will look like when I have finished!!

This morning, as I walked past the polo fields, not another person in sight. Often, you would see a lot of walkers, but today they are all either staying away because it is raining or simply not up and out yet.

When I reached the end of Cowdray, walking past the cafe and walk past the fabulous Easebourne church, you could head straight over and go up through Lime Avenue, which is a very pretty walk and if you're lucky, you can see the two Egyptian geese standing right at the top of one of the broken trees, talking to each other and putting the world to rights.

Something that I got remarkably familiar with when I used to walk that walk in the summer months when it was dry, but days like today where it has been raining, it does get particularly boggy and not very pleasant under foot.

Therefore, today I am going to the left a bit and walk past Easebourne shop and walk up the main road to the top towards Bexley Hill. Although this route still gets wet because the water from the top of Easebourne Street tends to gush down in a bit of a river at times, it will not be as muddy as walking through the Lime Avenue.

There are definitely a lot of holly berries out this year and maybe a sign that we will have a bad winter or just continue to be a wet one. Everywhere you look, you just see so many full holly trees stocked with the red berries, and I cannot actually remember seeing them so full in recent years.

One place that is always nice to see holly is as you walk up past the old Holly Tree pub. They have a fascinating holly tree there shaped to perfection and a slightly lighter colour holly, too. Walking past the old Easebourne school site, which is now being converted into houses, you can see the school's still remains untouched and you see the spire on the top with the clock and the weathervane showing North, East, South and West.

That is another place that holds a lot of special memories for me because both my sons went to that school before they moved to the new and current Easebourne Primary School. Lots of happy memories of school fetes, school discos and sports days.

As we continue up the street, we walked past the entrance to Love's Farm, which if you had walked on My Badger Walk you would come to the top of Loves Farm near to where the Bee Hives are. You find a lot of the routes I have walked entwine into each other, which is always good, because if I ever found myself wanting to extend my route I could combine other routes.

I am progressing with my confidence in my knowledge of the area, knowing where I am and where various paths take me to, so I am finding I am extending more of my routes, especially now with attempting the 800-mile Arctic Challenge. Coming up to the next tree, it is like a big elephant's trunk, with its leathery worn look, coming out of the ground. I can imagine putting two eyes on it to complete it.

This walk is always a good training walk for hill work, as it is one of those exceptionally long, never ending hills. As I venture up the hill, I found asking myself "how do slugs that are thick and fat manage to climb up one side of a very thin piece of grass without it bending, as they get right to the top and curl themselves over?" How is that possible?

Hearing and seeing the pheasants at this point as we reach the wooded section, where often you would see the deer hiding for protection. The coat's back off again as its hot walking up this hill. I personally hate wearing coats and have been like that since I was a child, and it is no wonder why I struggle to tell my younger son to keep putting his coat on too as I know how irritating it really is. If he is like me, which I am sure he is, in many ways, then he hates the restriction that a coat gives you. I would rather get slightly wet and be able to walk freely, but we are all different and unique.

Almost 2 hours in and I am still making my way up to the top of Easebourne Street near to Bexley Hill and I have hit the six miles point. This hill work is exceedingly difficult at times, and I keep telling myself to just keep putting one foot in front of the other and try to not to keep looking up as to where the top is.

If you get out of breath, just stop for a moment, something I was always ended up doing in the beginning of these hill walks, but overtime you find yourself getting further to the top before stopping. Trust me, I had questioned many of times, why I was doing what I was doing, walking my way up these hills but when you get to the top, you know why.

At the top we take a right heading down towards to Verdley Farm, and it is full of lots of pine trees in the distance and I can see they have been busy coppicing the chestnut ready for walking sticks.

The rain is getting a lot harder now and as we pass Verdley Farm on the right, it is always lovely to see the horses in the field grazing. Sometimes they come over and greet us, but today they are enjoying their food and who would blame them.

Although it is still raining there is a welcomed slight coverage from the trees, there are only a few flowers to look at due to the season, so just the greenery of all the holly and pine trees around me.

Life will be coming out very soon as we start to get out of Winter and enter into Spring, however as we are finding the seasons are changing with blooms making their way out earlier, anything is possible.

We have been walking just over the 7-mile mark now, according to my Strava, and stepping a lot on the banks this morning to let the cars through. Normally this is such a quite route but maybe there is an early morning shoot on today. There is a deluge of traffic cones stuck in the deep holes too, around the edges of the roads as they just are caving in everywhere around.

I am pleased to say that we have done the majority of the hill work now, just slight inclines to go as we walk up to Kings Drive and further up Scotland Lane before reaching the woods. Well, that made me jump!

A squirrel has jumped from one tree to another in front of me and Samo has nearly wrenched my arm off, thanks for that Samo, excellent job I have another one. He does love watching the squirrels as they scrabble up the pine trees, which you can see next to me on the left. There are rows and rows and of them, looking all uniformed and pretty spectacular, mind you on a dark night I can imagine they could be a bit spooky.

As I approach the 9-mile mark, venture up the track to the woodlands, it is absolutely plastered in mud from the rain and having a white dog when it is muddy is never a great idea. Forgetting how wet his lead was I threw it around my shoulders, and I now have the pleasure of a wet, sloppy lead around my neck, which is never the nicest feelings when you are walking, but the things you do when you have a dog.

As we start to turn to the direction of Older Hill the rain has continued to stop, and every now and then you just get the refreshing drips falling from the trees, which is actually quite nice as I got hot walking up those hills. They certainly make you tire easier, but I know there is a bench shortly to recover on as we look over the Surrey Hills.

But after that moment of thinking about that bench and the relief it would bring, there is nothing like a pickup to drive up the lane with its foot down, the exhaust smoking as you breathe in those pleasant vehicle fumes to put you off your thoughts. Just when you think you are in the country and escaping all of that traffic something like that happens.

We take a left down into the woods which takes us down to the setting of the Older Hill bench. Getting off that track was nice because it was full of muddy puddles, but actually it is still extremely muddy and slippery as we descend down now onto Older Hill. The walkway is full of bright yellow gorses which are beautiful but extremely sharp when you are walking past them.

In the distance, by the bench and the large tree overlooking the stunning views, I can see the delight of the Belted Galloways watching my every move. There is one over by a tree scratching his head against the trunk, with what looks to be a serious itch on his neck.

Then there is another one trying to chew the bark or leaves off the lower tree, and we have got one to the right of us that is lifting its neck right up like a giraffe trying to eat the leaves high off the trees.

Then the other two are in the middle showing their affection and grooming each other. They have bells on their neck so they can be heard, and it was such a wonderful sight to see, and it has certainly made my wet 3 hour walk today.

Now it was time to turn around, I cannot spend all day looking at the cows. We are greeted at the top of this small track before heading back down to the common by a Serpent Carving, which is part of the Serpent Trail Route that I did a while back. In fact, it was one of the longest walks that I have ever done, but a remarkably interesting and rewarding one.

I can hear a tractor coming up the track behind us and it slowly progresses with some silage on the back as you get that whiff as it passes through. I had to let him pass by diving in the woods, because the roads are not big enough for the two of us and he is a bit bigger than I am.

As I head back down through Woolbeding Common I hit the 10-mile mark. I know by the time I get back home; it could be a 13 or 14 mile route today, which is certainly a lovely start to the day.

I will certainly be looking forward to some breakfast when I get back. I feel so alive, and invigorated by this walk this morning and its certainly one of those days that you could just keep on walking and walking. I have days like that. Knowing I have done the hard part of all the hills and on a route downhill enjoying the descent through the heather lands is why. It is so pretty, with all the vibrant colours of the heathers coming out. The purples, the yellows, and the whites and all the greenery, you can see for miles.

Must be to do with the endorphins that walking releases that gives you that bounce and boost in your step. When I hit that 10-mile mark even though my legs may feel tired and hips start to ache, I also am refreshed with this new energy.

I just feel like I can tackle anything today. Ready to bring what comes my way head strong. These are the moments that I realise just why I am doing the walking and remember just how much it really does lift your spirits and you can cope with what is going on.

The amount of time I have spent with just myself in nature has really helped me mentally deal with everything that has been going on with my grandad too. Times have been really hard at the moment and being out in the fresh air, amongst the trees and the birds, with only the odd person to say good morning to as you walk past them as they are cycling, running, or walking their dog, its clear space to process your mind and your thoughts. It is also time though where you end up learning so much more about yourself and what you are capable of and what your strengths are. Just when you think you want to give up, turn around and go home, you see something that inspires you and you end up carrying on.

It was only a few hours ago I was lying in bed thinking, I do not want to get out of bed. I am all tucked up here, nice, and warm.

I could have quite easily turned over and gone back to sleep, but I am so glad I pushed myself out and made that decision to turn off that alarm and get up and get out before anyone stirred.

I feel absolutely great and, as I say, ready to tackle anything headstrong today. So, as I descend home, it is muddy and slippery, but I have my waterproof socks, and gaiters on to help minimise my wet feet. I walk out to Woolbeding past the National Trust Gardens, which has now a contemporary glasshouse set amongst its countryside views, shaped like a diamond it really is spectacular.

Continuing down to the bridge and back on the main road I decided to head back to Bepton so I could boost my mileage and get closer to my 800-mile target. I was at about 225 miles in and still away to go but I still had weeks left so was not panicking just yet. As I get home,

I had hit fifteen miles and walked just over 5 hours and was happy with my achievement today.

January 24 - 'Never believe the Weatherman Walk'.

Levin Down, Cocking, Charlton & West Dean - 16km (10 miles)

So, this morning I've chosen to do a route which starts off at Cocking Hill, at the car park by the Cadence Cafe. On my own today, I ventured up the top of Cocking Hill on the same route I took when I ventured here for my first ever 10-mile walk. But as I reached the large marker stone, by the signposts, I took a left down to West Dean Woods which would then take me on to Singleton before making my way over to Charlton and back through to Cocking.

I was hoping that this would take me about 3.5 hours today, it was a particularly frosty and foggy morning, and I could see my breath as I marched my way up the hill, but hopefully it will turn out to be a wonderful day, well that's what the weather man said anyway.

I have woken up this morning really struggling with pains in my elbows, wrists and my neck, something that I often have a battle with particularly when it is cold and damp. I put it down at first to the Raynaud's, which can cause an awful lot of joint pain, but also now it is to do with my EDS and recent diagnosis of degenerative discs, and arthritis in my neck.

It is on days like this you have got to really push yourself hard as, it would be quite easy to say, no, I am not going to do something today, I am in too much pain, but I am not letting this pain defeat me.

Walking does help me partly because I think once you are out in nature you can forget what is going on with your body and take in what is around you. It helps the arthritis in my hips too as keeping walking seems to keep it from settling in my joints, but I really do feel it if I do not get out, which is why I continue, almost scared sometimes what would happen if I stopped.

This morning the path is damp and very slippery on the flints and the chalk. I am absolutely sure this route was the cause of my very first toenail loss, because what you find is after you have been walking a few hours, you do not pick up your feet as you should, and you start dragging them.

As I reach the large stone where normally I would continue straight up the top of the hill, I branched left towards the woodlands of great pine trees. It was just under the mile to get to this point and 20 minutes walking up the hill, but it is such a relief when you get to the top. The views are really spectacular. You can look down and see the main road where everyone is travelling on their day.

But as I say today, all you can see is the thick fog as it lies over the hills with a view of the forever green trees to the woods on the left-hand side of me. They have been doing a lot of tree work at the moment, removing the old, I assume, ash trees and thinning out the woods but with that comes the deep wet ruts where the big trucks have been going in and out, which has made it extremely hard walking especially as the rain has been belting down recently too.

I love walking in the rain, just hate at times the muddy conditions it leaves making walking so much harder and slower. So far on my 800-mile challenge, the majority of it has been in wet muddy conditions which has not been the most pleasant at times, but I always try to find the positives. There is something about walking when you're cosy and dry, where you just hear that pitter patter on your hood or your cap of the rain droplets, and you watch them fall onto the leaves, watching that leaf bends down with the weight of the drop, there's just something magical about that sheer moment in time.

Walking is so good for your health, and I have finally managed to get my work & life balance right. In the beginning I used to feel extremely guilty for taking that time out. Very guilty that I was not, I suppose, there at everyone's disposal. It felt selfish because I was taking a couple of hours out for me, and it felt wrong, which was hard to process in the beginning.

I worried about what everyone was thinking, questioning me for what I am doing and why I am able to be out in nature so much? But actually, I have learned to realise that it actually does not matter what other people think. This is what I am doing for me, it is me that matters and it is me that is doing it. I am not slacking on any of my work, I am not missing deadlines, I am not doing things that I should not be doing, I am still getting everything done, even though I am taking time out for myself.

It's a really, really important lesson that I have learnt and being able to share and hopefully help someone else having that same mental block that I did, well then that is an achievement too. We here to help each other in life.

Carrying on further into the woods, I come across a little woods department set in the heart of the woods with an old-fashioned tractor and a seat carved out of a wood stump. The logs are piled high in their various thicknesses of trees and a little old trailer is buried in the woodland.

A pretty little area, and as I look up into one of the trees there is a big bird box sat up there, which I wonder if it is for the owls to go in. Often you can hear them in the woods early in the morning, but I have never as yet had that pleasure of seeing one. So, we go through into the West Dean Estate I continue down further into the woods, and I can hear the rain up above. It is only spitting at this point, so hopefully I will get all the way around before we have the deluge of rain that is not meant to be coming in till after 1pm.

With the pinecones dotted around all over the floor the route becomes once again muddy and slippery. I have been walking for just over 2 hours and walked just under 5km, and approaching an opening out of the woods where it is full of fields everywhere you look. In the summer these are filled with rapeseed and everywhere you look is bright, bright yellow.

At this turning point too, if you turned right, you could do a route round to Chilgrove and back over the fields and hills back on the track to Cocking, which is also a nice route to walk. But today I am carrying on and going down a farm track where there is a lovely little house on the left-hand side of me.

They have been planting lots of trees along the side of the headlands and they are all wrapped up in the plastic coving, to protect them from the nibbling deer, which I have not seen yet any today. Often in the woods, you can see the little muntjac deer or hear them rustling in the distance. The rain is really getting heavy now as I approach a farm area before we then descend down into Singleton.

People are banging around in the background, and you can see the old JCB working as I walked through the farm. Making my way down to the left by a couple of houses, to the right there is a field where last time I saw a number of horses grazing but today the field is empty.

As I make my way over a stile and through the field, back over another stile, I approach the edge of a woodland that is very overgrown with brambles and stingers, but I make my way through it and up to the top of the hill where you can look into the distance and see Goodwood Race Circuit and the pylons on top of the trundle.

I descend down over the hill, which is a hill that I have got to be careful on because I have slipped down there when it has been wet in the past. I then head down towards the cricket field in Singleton. A reminder of those Sundays I would be making the cricket teas with my mum and nan as a small child, and then watching my grandad play and then umpire, something that meant a lot to our family as they were all involved in some way.

Straight over the main road I headed through the pretty little village of Singleton, making my way up to the little village church and then alongside the playground into a field. A reminder that ticks where in the field so luckily had my trousers on as did not want to go through all that again, and I did make sure to check myself after the walk as they have a habit of gripping on where you least expect it. Setting off through this beautiful meadow field, the views over the hills were so pretty and I could see in the distance the hill I would be making my way up to when I found myself in Charlton within a few minutes time.

Heading down through the farm I came across a sign telling me there were free range chickens running around the farm and a cattle truck was coming down the lane, where two farmers were waiting their arrival. I knew why as I could hear this humongous stunning bull in the field above, mooing its little heart out as his females where on the way!

Venturing back through the woods heading back up to the top of Cocking Hill I was absolutely drenched and covered in mud. Today I was not getting away with being soaked all the way through to my underwear! I was certainly unprepared for today's weather as on my weather app it said it was dry till later this afternoon, how wrong was I.

Walking back down the hill towards my car, the water was running down the hill like a river where I was walking, and I was like a duck waddling through and as I got to the bottom to finish my walk just as I approached the main road a lovely car decided to splash me in the huge puddle, probably giggling at the state of me. At this point I had gone beyond caring as I was soaked anyway and was glad to get home, get showered and in warm clothes.

I do love walking in the rain, but today tested that and the love slightly went from love to just enjoyment, but as I have said before it is all creating memories, getting out, and doing yourself and your mind good. If we kept walking to just the nice days, I am sure half the year we would not step outside! My tip would just be always prepared, taking a waterproof coat in your rucksack for those unexpected weather moments, then it will save you from getting completely soaked. Partly wet is better than fully!

February 24 – 'The Chinook Walk'

Midhurst to Chichester Circular - 41km (26 Miles)

Waking up one February morning, I thought I am in the mood for a challenge and fancied the idea of walking to Chichester Cathedral with the aim of catching the bus home. So, rucksack on all stocked up and walking boots laced up, I headed out the door making my way down to West Lavington and on to the Heyshott Roughs which I had done many of times before.

As I approached the village of Heyshott I headed to the back of the village hall where a footpath took me across a field and over to the bottom of a hill. The grand Heyshott Hill that from the road did not look too bad. Well looking up at that hill as I was stood at the bottom, I started to have seconds thoughts about what I had let myself in for. It really was a steep hill, but convinced myself I could do it.

Somehow with complete determination that I was not going to be defeated this early on in the day, I dug deep to find that hidden strength within me to walk my way up that hill, thinking it really was never going to end.

Stopping 7 or 8 times to reach the top, it is one of the hardest hills I have combated to date, partly because of the steepness but also the muddy, slippery paths and loose gravel.

But I succeeded and that is what the adventure it about. Its believing in yourself that you can do it, and the achievement I feel once you reach the top is a feeling you cannot explain.

After I had caught back my breath, I then headed through the East Dean Woods which was lovely as it was all downhill from there, where I made my way to Charlton, stopping at the Fox Goes Free Pub for a coffee and a toilet stop.

Preparing myself for more hills, I knew that the next part of the route was to walk up to Goodwood, which also meant walking up to the trundle. I had already managed one huge hill, how am I going to cope with more, plus I did not have Samo with me today to pull me up on the lead.

You just keep putting one foot in front of the other and as you start looking around at the spectacular views you can stop concentrating on the hills and your hips, or lower back pain which gets me now.

When I crossed the top of Goodwood Hill you could see Chichester in the distance, that incredible spire of the cathedral, and I continued walking down hills where I ended up joining the Centurion Way. What a fantastic walk that was with the little models of the little armed guards made out of metal as you ventured the trail. They are full of such character and really make you smile.

I remember getting into Chichester and thinking, wow, I have done that in just under four and a half hours, something I was not prepare for of walking so quickly. I felt so energised and really on top of the world that I decided after a sandwich and drink I would walk back, like you do. I had plenty of time and did not need to be back at a specific time, I knew I had my essential battery pack to recharge my phone, as well as enough supplies to get me back so that is what I did.

This time I ventured back a slightly different route, which I went on again with a friend later on in this year. Walking back on the Centurion Way Trail walking to Brandy Hill Copse, with some fifteen acres of woodlands and three ponds, you were greeted with fantastic metal carvings of medieval characters on your way.

Not forgetting to stop of course for a few selfies with the tin men! The skies where blue and the sun was shining, and I made my way under a bridge surrounded with bright green foliage.

Following the trail with squirrels jumping from tree to tree I made my way up the trail until it took me to West Dean School. The fields in the distance where being prepared for crops by the farmers, and not the normal corn and wheat I was used to seeing in the summer months.

Walking then on through West Dean Woods where I had ventured many times before when I did the Charlton and Levin Down Route, I came across the Woods tractor in his exact same spot as I had seen it the month before.

At this point I was really questioning what I had done as my legs and hips were starting to fail me, by this time I had done just under twenty miles, and I could really feel it. I was starting to slow down too and knew I had about another 6 or 7 miles till I was home.

As I approached out of the woods which were so muddy and slippery, the sun was still beaming, but starting to lose its heat as it was approaching 4pm. I will still so hot as my body had warmed to much from the mileage I had walked.

This was certainly knocking up the mileage for my 800-mile challenge though which as this point I only had about 250 more to complete and just over 1 month to do it.

Once I had reached the top of Cocking Hill, my legs almost started to give in and my energy supplies where almost empty, probably because I knew exactly where I was and just how far I still had to go. I really did not know how I was ever going to walk my way back to Midhurst, yes, I could have waited for the bus, but I had got so far, I really did not want to be defeated, it is not in my nature.

Walkers are all different and for me when I am walking in places where I have not been before I seem to be more energetic, not knowing what to expect and you take every step with more passion as it is a new adventure, something I have loved about my journey.

But when you have walked from Cocking to Midhurst repeatedly, you know how far it is. At this point I was at the 20-mile point and flashbacks came of the amazing day that Jane and I walked our way back from Chichester and as soon as we reached the top of Cocking Hill, we had the most spectacular showdown of a Chinook flying overhead.

For about 15 minutes it was flying above our heads, heading one way, then heading back the other way over our heads again, looking like they were practicing for emergency drops. I absolutely love Chinooks, and this has certainly made this walk memorable and every time now I walk this part of the South Downs Way, I remember this showdown.

Heading down the flinty track taking extra care not to stub my toes again as I have already lost 2 toenails on my journeys so far, this walk just seemed to be no closer to ending and I thought I had actually taken on a challenge that I would not be able to complete. My feet and hips were aching, my knees were sore, and I was so hot.

I grabbed another coffee from The Country Inn on the way and managed to crawl back home, must have been that caffeine boost. I had done it, not sure how but I did. I was so proud of myself for not giving up and completely flopped once I got home.

Removing my KT tape off my toes both my feet and legs at the bottom were swollen and red, like they often are when I have done a longer walk.

My hands were so puffy, I could hardly bend my fingers, and although I have tried walking, holding my arms up in the air and shaking them around like they suggest doing, holding on to your rucksack, nothing seemed to work.

Stocking up on pasta that evening, plenty of fluids to rehydrate I had walked twenty-six miles in just over 9 hours and was beaming with self-achievement. Pushing yourself certainly has rewards that no one can take away from you as you did it yourself and that is worth so much.

March 24 – 'Caught by the Delivery Driver Walk'

Cocking & Bepton Circular - 14km (9 miles)

Within the second week of March, I had completed my 800-mile training walk so could scale down on my walks now to prepare me for the next few weeks when I would be taking on my next challenge.

A route which now I probably do weekly as part of my training, is a 14km route heading from home over the Midhurst Common, to The Country Inn, Bepton to pick up my coffee and cookie, I head down to the Midhurst Brickworks, before heading out on the main A272, walking down to Cocking then back through the back lanes to Bepton and back home.

Walking through the brickworks at this time of year, you would have all the little lambs dotted around with their mums. A lovely sound, hearing them bleat and jump and see them being so happy, jumping for joy. As the mum watches us, concerned, the little lambs show their little tails wiggling around as they were trying to get milk off their mum. Always so nice to see them in the fields and such a refreshing time, lambing time, seeing the new life coming into this world.

Further down the lane as we walk past the farm and houses, we approach further down the track, beautiful horses in the fields. This walk was always a walk where you would see lots of animals. Later on in the walk, you often see the alpacas or llamas, not sure which one they are in the fields on the Bepton straight.

As I head down the thin pathway heading back down towards Cocking, the route can become a bit noisy with the cars and tractors flying by.

But once you get back on to the country lanes, heading back towards Bepton your back in the presence of the hills in the distance, those hills I now look up at and think I have walked them so many times and not sure how I have ever done it as from the bottom they look so high.

Making my way through the winding roads back to Bepton, you would often see the kites flowing overhead circling, looking for their catch of the day.

They were always something that I wish I had a better camera to photograph them with, because they are such beautiful birds with their fork tails, and I always felt privileged to see these birds.

Making a quick dash into a field for a wee, which is unfortunately something you have to get used to as walking on these long routes unfortunately toilets aren't often provided, I found what I thought was a safe spot, away from view. I could hear a van stop, and I thought 'oh no, quick, someone's going to catch me with my trousers down. I listened as the driver's door opened, trying to be quiet, I waited and then heard the door shut and the driver go off.

The relief I had that I didn't get caught out but then just as I thought I was in the clear as I ventured back onto the track, coming out of the field, a friend went by in their car, looking over and waving. My face probably went bright red and I saw them later that day saying, I am sure that wasn't a footpath where you were walking!! And that was it I was caught out by that call of nature!!

Walking back down past the Park House Hotel back to Bepton is always a nice refreshing walk, downhill but one of those long roads that never seems to end, but with the coffee stop in sight, you continue and before you know it you are back.

The views on the way back at this time of year are fantastic, the flowers are all coming out in bloom, you can hear the baby lambs in the distance and a peaceful route back home. I love this route and I continue to do this weekly as one of my training routes as I prepare for my new Ultra Challenges.

Over the months that I have walked it, I have seen the change in seasons, watching the sun come up and go down over the fields, seeing the little lambs as they are born, and in the freezing winter you watch the sun glisten off the frosty fields and fences.

But there is so much more for me to discover, and I am extremely excited about all the new paths I have yet to adventure on. My walks have been around the South Downs so far and I am looking forward to exploring new routes as I continue to walk. This is what my journey has been about and preparing me for my new Ultra Challenges.

On the 26th of March, we had the most devasting news. My grandad had become extremely poorly overnight and was admitted into hospital at Chichester, where after various tests and scans they had said that he would unfortunately not get through this serious infection, and it was time to consider end of life care.

We managed to get him back to Rotherlea where he received his end-of-life care, staying with him overnight, throughout the day, just popping back home for a quick bite to eat every now and then, the next 2 weeks leading up to my next Ultra Marathon were the hardest 2 weeks of my life.

My world was starting to crumble as I always believed that nothing could take my grandad away from me, that he would go on forever. I had one of my biggest events coming up as yet that I had taken on and at the same time I had the biggest emotional event to deal with too. I just did not know how I was going to get through this. My world felt like it was ending.

As I look back now, I realise that this was grandads' way of making sure that I rested completely, no walking before my Ultra Challenge, which you were advised to do, as I stayed with him, being told on several occasions that today could be the day we said goodbye.

But he kept fighting as he knew on the 6th of April 24, I would be taking on my next Ultra Marathon Challenge for MacMillan Cancer Support and he wanted to be with me by my side. And he was…

April 24 - 'Walking with my Heart'

My 2nd Ultra Marathon – Easter Thames Path for Macmillan Cancer - 50km – (31 miles)

It's the 6 April 2024, 4am and my alarm clock goes off ready for my adventures today. Travelling to Windsor to take on my 50km Easter Challenge around the Thames Path for MacMillan Cancer Research.

Today I was walking for the four ladies in my life that inspired me and gave me strength, all who had battled cancer. My dear Mum who 3 years ago underwent treatment for Ovarian Cancer. My dear friend and employee Amber who at the same time my journey started was undergoing and continues treatment for Breast Cancer.

My friend Emma who continues with the aftereffects of her Bowel Cancer treatment and whom I will be eternally grateful for her openness and conversations that got me to where I am today. And not forgetting my amazing cousin Sharlene, who through all her battles, sadly lost her life back in 2020 to Breast Cancer, but in her journey showed such strength and determination, love and care for others even whilst she battled with a nasty aggressive form of cancer.

So, an emotional day ahead, knowing that my battles today would be nothing compared to what these ladies and many others everyday deal with through their Cancer Journey. I had finally arrived at Windsor, and after being prepared the night before ready for the day ahead, my challenge was about to commence. I was excited but also exhausted as the days leading up to this day had been quite difficult.

With my grandad being very poorly and receiving end of life care, part of me did not want to leave him and not do the challenge, but I knew he would want me to continue, despite what was happening with him, he knew I had worked so hard to get ready for this event.

The night before the event I had managed a few hours' sleep which was needed as during the last 2 weeks I was running on adrenaline; a lack of sleep is obviously not a clever idea when you are about to embark on an Ultra-Marathon. But I was determined that I was going to get around before he passed away and get back to him with my medal. That was the focus of my walk, it was getting around, enjoying the moments and being back to him as soon as I could with the news that I had completed it.

To be honest, it is exactly what I had needed at that point, because for many days, I had not left his bedside, only for short periods of time.

So, this was very much a healing walk at the same time as a hard emotional walk. I needed to absorb the fresh air and process all that had been going on, because it had been a complete whirlwind since he had been into hospital two weeks prior.

Once I had arrived and pulled up into the car park it was about a ten-minute walk down to the starting point and they had marked out arrows to take you there. Within a few minutes of walking, I had started to walk down the wrong way, so I thought this was going to be an interesting challenge if I was diverting before even crossing that start line!!

Flying overhead I could see and hear the massive jumbos coming into land or taking off from the airport close by. I signed in and received my pack with my number 1344, it was all real now, I am taking on the full 50 km challenge and I sat waiting for the warmup to commence with a much-needed boost of caffeine!

There were quite a few people here ready to start the 8:00am challenge with me and it was a beautiful sunny day, not too hot at this point, but I was expecting it to be quite warm later in the day. After the rain that we had had previously, it was a joy to see the sunshine.

The warmup took place and then the countdown began: 5, 4, 3, 2, 1 and we are off. I had started walking the figure of eight route heading firstly to Old Windsor and then on towards Runnymede before heading back to the start at Windsor Racecourse, where I would have lunch and then start the second part.

So, firstly I walked by this commemorative Spitfire on the left before heading towards the riverside. The sun was just lifting and was reflecting on the water, and you could see the many swans as they were just calmly swimming towards us. A lot of them had little babies on the side and wherever you looked, you just saw beautiful swans. I had come up over to a bridge, and even going up and down the steps seemed quite an effort so I knew it was going to be a long day. As I walked down by a playing field as you turned around, you could see Windsor Castle behind you, a fantastic view.

Carrying on up and down over a railway crossing bridge, over a playing field then onto the Thames Walk path, which to this point had been tarmac pathways, I had come to my first muddy section where it had been very wet during the build up to this walk. I knew they had rerouted, which I was expecting as the Ultra-Challenge team often do to make it safe for everyone. However, they would never take any kms off, they always add them on.

You know, with your challenges when you are out for a 50km, it is always going to be 50km plus something. Well, it was on my Strava and Fitbit Apps, but I know these are always not a true reckoning on the mileage!

Managing to stay on two feet at this point I was pleased I had avoided face planting the mud, which for me was always tricky!! Back on the road, walking on tarmac which a lot of this route was (thankfully I had done plenty of road training as this can make such a difference to your feet), I came out next to a section where I saw a turning right to Windsor and left to Staines 7 miles, Old Windsor 2 and this is where the markers were set out with their bright pink arrows.

Heading down Windsor Road towards Old Windsor I had come to a beautiful archway bridge, which they had rerouted through to the left, as the right side was quite deep in water, so I was not going to have to get my wellies out for this part!! Mind you not that I had any, I was planning on my Sealskinz Waterproof Socks to help me out with the wet parts!

As I continued down the waterway side and reaching the 8km sign, then the 9km, I kept carrying on speaking to a couple along the way, which always helped give you a motivational boost. The next part of the route took you past some beautiful large houses, set on the river's edge with all their boats moored outside their gardens. What a place to live.

Then I passed to the right the old Harvester Restaurant that I remember taking the boys to when I visited Legoland many years ago and remember sitting in there at 10:00pm at night, waiting to get food and enjoying the views over the water. It was a lovely memory that I had forgotten about, and it is amazing how you can bring yourself back to that moment in time.

As I went past the 10km sign, knowing that soon it would be the first stop point, passing the roundabout towards Staines and Egham, which eventually took you down to Runnymede, where I continued walking to the first stop. I came across this incredible statue, which I think must have been the statue that is on everyone's phone at this point, of Queen Elizabeth II, which was unveiled on the 14 June 2015 by the Rifle Honourable John Barrow, MP, Member of Parliament in Buckingham and Speaker of the House of Commons in presence of the High Sheriff of Surrey, and Ms Elizabeth Kennedy, the Mayor of Runnymede. Such a beautiful statue to see as I approached the first stop.

At this point I sent a video for my grandad which I sent onto my mum as she was by his side, so he could hear that I had reached my first stop. Throughout the day on my walk, I was sending updates because I wanted grandad to hang in there until I got back. Although we do not know at that stage whether he could hear, hopefully hearing my voice would help him, to know that I was still with him.

It also helped me to be doing that, knowing that I could still be with him, even though I was far away.

Enjoying some lovely peanuts and a banana and a cup of coffee, I grabbed myself a couple of bags of Haribo's to then enjoy on the next stage where I continued walking up the side of the Thames with the river on the left. Then I came across the hill of hell that everyone had been talking about. I knew there was only one hill in this route, but oh yes, it was a hill. Before I had got to the hill, you had to walk across a field and a lot of it was dry paths but then as I turned to the right, it then became a very boggy marsh. Yes, me, being me, you guessed it I did go down on my knees, but luckily managed to put my fingers down, so I did not get my face into it.

I remember two behind me giggling to themselves, checking I was all right, and I said, *"don't laugh, you could be the next one, there are bound to be others, I am sure!* "So, yes, lovely muddy knees and feet before I took on the hill of hell and at times, I really wanted to stop up this hill, but I knew if I stopped, I would struggle to get going again.

Remembering again what my great friend Jane had told me when struggling up hills and to take the pressure of your knees and hips, walk up diagonally which I did and managed to get to the top finally.

As I reached the top, I started speaking to a lovely guy from Newcastle who was also a solo walker like me, and we chatted for a bit which helped me get through the next phase. He had recently lost his dad and had done lots of walks on his own too and he mentioned that he would be walking over the South Downs Way at some point to go and scatter his dad's ashes, as that is a place that his dad loved. He had not been down that way, so he was very much looking forward to doing that this year.

You meet so many nice people on these challenges and it is one of the nicest things about these events is that everyone is so uplifting and wants everyone else to succeed. People support each other, complete strangers but by the end you make new friends. There is always someone there when you are struggling. There is always someone in front, or behind, or to the side of you. You can talk to people when you get to the stops, or chat to them on the way as you walk, they are such well organised stops too, they have got all the facilities there and the drinks, the food, the toilets, and the staff if you need them.

As I walked, I remember thinking how these Ultra Challenges have helped me so much. Not only have they given me a new life and purpose, but they definitely were also the way that I can do something for others.

Each walk that I did was not only for myself, but it was a way to raise money for various charities, giving something back to those that had helped my family too. I had already done the Dementia UK charity in September 23, doing the South Coast Ultra Marathon, and I raised over £1500 pounds. So far, I had raised over a £1000 for Macmillan doing this walk today and this is what is getting me through these hard parts of the walk.

Heading back into the moment and I was carrying on into Windsor Great Park and I saw three lovely white horses in front of me as I approached the entrance to the park and the start of the famous mile. I had just approached the 18km point and I had been warned that this was like a two-and-a-half-mile stroll not the mile that it has its name of.

Turning around and taking a photo of the big statue on the hill and then looking forward as to how far it was in the distance to the next point, I was shocked. You actually could not see where we were heading for it was that long, but such a, privileged beautiful walk.

I felt very honored to be walking up this walk, as you often see it on the television for royal weddings, funerals, and events. So much history has taken place right here on this walk. The path never seemed to end, and I remember saying to myself *"just keep walking, keep walking, put one foot in front of the other and you will get to the end."*

I walked and I walked, and although it has only a very slight incline on it, it was enough that you could feel every footstep. It is one of those never-ending roads that you look back and you are halfway between it and just seemed to keep going and going and going.

But finally, eventually I managed to get to the end with the golden topped gates before venturing into the part of the town where there were some very, very posh cars. Looking for the signs, I started again to walk off in a different direction before realising I was off route and made a quick turn back before anyone noticed.

Then approaching the route where I had started from, I came to the second checkpoint. At this point, I was really starting to feel it, I had that fuzzy tingling in my nose and needed food and drink. But first it was time to completely change my clothes and footwear before getting supplies.

I had put my change bag in the bag hold system which was extremely helpful to have a change of clothes there ready for you. At this point, I was not wearing any plasters on my feet because I had covered them in Gerwhol cream and touch wood this has been my savior when I have been doing long walks. I found that after a while, the KT tape, was becoming irritated on my skin and I did not know whether that was causing what my legs to swell.

I layered my feet in a layer of the cream, and it was smothered in white grease which obviously helps cause less friction which in turn causes the sores and blisters and it was working for me. I put my new pair of fresh socks on, which, must admit, felt fantastic. Just to get my toes out in the fresh air was amazing. I did apply a large plaster around my big toe, because I have been starting to lose my big toe now for a while and did not want this one to be the final straw, to have that come off while I was walking.

After putting on a new pair of boots, I questioned whether I had done the right thing as it took a while for my feet to adjust in a slightly different pair of boots. They did not feel quite the same at first but as I started back on my way for the next 25km they were fine. So, I squeezed everything back in the bag, handed it back to the team and grabbed myself a lovely cheese roll, banana, coke, and some crisps to keep me going and off again I went eating on the way as I did not want to sit down too long and seize up.

Part 2 took my back on the route I had started but turning a different way walking under a different bridge. There was a magnificent graffiti image. It was, humongous, and done in black and white, with a range of people's faces with random expressions and tongues sticking out, smiling and laughing and absolutely wonderful to see.

These artists are so talented and so clever. I continued walking; the sun was still shining, and I had come across a piece of water which looked like it was being used for canoe training. I had just reached the 30 km point and I was starting to slow down now, the walk was getting tiring, but I knew I still had 20km to go. Walking away from the water now, walking up some fenced areas with some tall trees, gravel paths, and walking around to another bridge, crossing the road, and seeing the 36 km was delightful. I could start on my countdown of Kms.

I came face to face with a humongous, beautiful white swan, one of the route masters in disguise I am sure, he was placed there with his big orange beak and these large leathery feet just standing there looking at me.

I headed back on the route that was taking us back round now to where we had already walked before, to get us back to the finish line. There was this little beautiful white pony behind some coppice fencing and honestly, it really just needed a unicorn's horn to complete it. It was just a magical white pony that looked like it was a unicorn in disguise.

It was just starting to cloud over, and I walked back under the bridge that I had walked previously. So, the water was now on the right-hand side as I ventured back and coming up to the 40km I was really, really, really struggling. I had my kind friend Jane sending me messages throughout the day, just trying to keep me boosted, as, she knew how hard it was for me. This walk, particularly with what had been going on with my grandad, had made it even harder.

She said to me, *"not long to the pick a mix stop now"* and I said, *"I'm almost there just 2 km to go, but at this point it was the hardest 2km of the route"*. I was really struggling, and I had hit the wall at this point. I knew that I had to just keep continuing with one foot in front of the other, my hip was starting to struggle, my knee was giving me a few niggles and I was tired, really, really tired.

At this point, I knew I had only 10 km to get back, which was another couple of hours walking and it seemed impossible. At this point I had already walked 9 hours, so I was very tired, but I really did not want to give up.

But I got to the next stop by the canal lock at 42km and I could see the third checkpoint. I have never been so excited to see a pick a mix store where there was yellow bananas and liquorice allsorts, and pink shrimps and white and yellow milk bottles. I have never rammed so many sweets in one of those little pink and white stripy bags that you used to get from the sweet shop if you were good. This was really my saving point.

At this point I waited and saw the physios because I was really, really struggling with my knee and I was a bit concerned about whether I would be able to continue and get to that finish line. So, I waited to see the physio and then smothered my knee in cold ice spray because at that point I had already taken some anti-inflammatories so I could not take any more. There was not a lot that they could do at that particular stop, so I continued putting one foot in front of the other, concentrating on my sweets rather than thinking about the 8km that I had to go back.

It had clouded over a bit and there were a few spots of rain, but at that point I was so hot that it did not bother me. It was actually quite nice to have a bit of wet to cool me down. The sun was pitching through the clouds and reflecting on the side of the water and these huge geese were talking away to themselves on the side of the river and I was just approaching the 44 km part and I was struggling, with another 6 km to go.

This point, it was really, really hard to carry on but kept thinking about my grandad and getting back for him and also reminding myself as to why I was doing this walk, for Macmillan Cancer, and when times were tough for my friends and family fighting cancer, they couldn't stop they had to carry on whatever pain and discomfort they were going through.

So, I kept trying to stay positive and concentrated on the beautiful swans and geese around me. The sun was going down and I thought, well, it is not going to be long now before it gets dark.

My aim was to get back before 7:00 pm so I could start heading back to pick up my medal and get back to grandad. I looked over in the distance and I could see the finish line and I somehow managed to drag myself over it not actually believing I had done it. I was a finisher. I had actually finished my 2nd Ultra Marathon and at that moment I beamed with glory.

But I also, at that point, fell apart. My knee and hip crumbled. I tried to drag myself over to get my bag, but I needed to see the physio first and I sat there and explained what the problem was? She looked at my legs and halfway up my leg above my ankles it looked, as if someone had poured boiling water over them, they were so sore, red, and swollen. It is a thing I get a lot more of now when I am walking.

"We'll get you some hydrocortisone cream to apply to that, to try and take it down and cool it off a bit" she said. I then saw one of the physios which I am sure had been so busy with all of us walkers but so great to have them onsite to help you. I had tightened my calves so much that everything was pulling in the wrong places. I had just overdone it, and my legs were saying please no more. They just could not take it and was just shutting things down to say stop now please. My calves were so tight, and it was pulling on my knee and my tendons.

So, after about 20 minutes of physio, I think it did help a little bit, I managed to get back up and sort of hobble over to get my bag and belongings. I knew, although I did not want to eat at this point, I just wanted to get back in the car and get home I had to get myself something to eat and drink, to start to repair my body for what it had just been put through. 10 hrs. 46 minutes of walking!!

I had picked up my medal and t-shirt and I just wanted to get back for my grandad, but I had to be put my sensible hat on and I got a plate of Bolognese and rice and a can of Pepsi to keep me going.

Then off I went heading back out the start line back to get my car. I remember what took me 10 minutes to get to the start line before, took me 30 minutes to hobble back to the car park. I was in tears. On my Strava it said I had walked 68,292 steps.

I had been walking for 10 hours, 46, and mileage was thirty-nine miles. This was my walking all day so included my pre and post event and I just could not believe what I had done. I was so proud of myself and hoped that my grandad would be proud too as I was doing this for him as well as my girls. I had got back in the car and my focus now was getting out of Windsor.
Well, that was the joy, I think, when you are tired and you are not sure where you are going, it becomes so much harder. I drove around that roundabout four times before picking the right exit point. I wanted to get back to Petworth, Rotherlea and put the medal in grandads' hand before he passed.

And I had achieved it. I spoke to Grandad, whether he could hear me or not and I sat with him, holding his hand, at this point I was running on so much adrenaline. Three days later, on April 9th Grandad sadly passed away while we were beside his bed. He was such a strong man and that day he gave me that strength to undertake that Ultra Marathon and get back for him.

Every future walk now I will have that memory with me of crossing that finish line and getting that medal. Now not only will that medal be for me, but that medal will be for my grandad too. And although he will not be here to hold my hand and hold my medal with me, he will be with me in my heart, close by on my future walks. This is a day that I will never forget. I did it. I did a 50 km walk, my second ultra challenge and already I have booked my third, in July 24, the North Downs Walk for my grandad.

The moment I will treasure forever – the day I walked back into Rotherlea to give my grandad my medal before he passed.

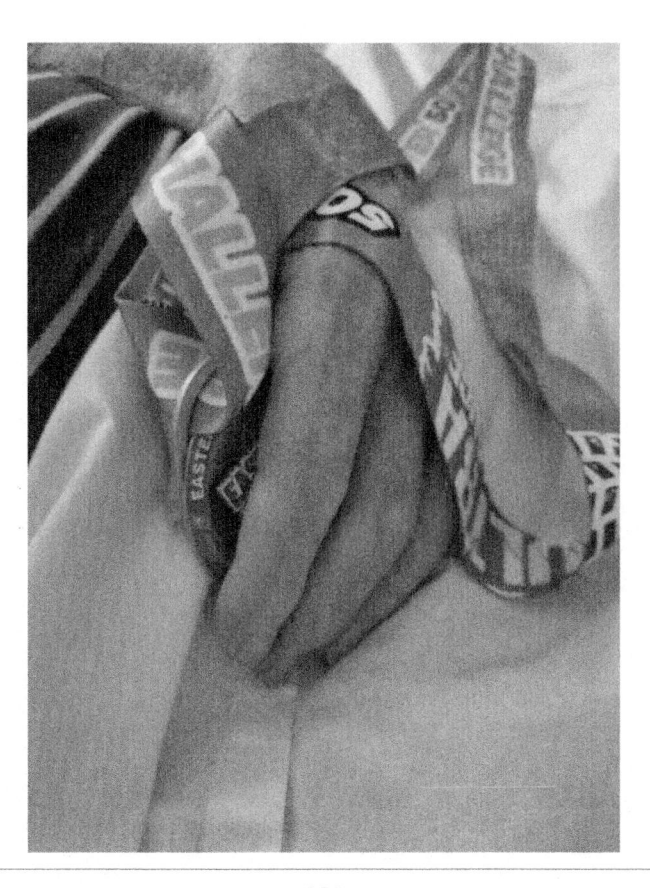

My Future Adventures & Challenges ...

After my grandad had passed back in April 24, I'd somehow not only lost one of the greatest men I have known, but I'd lost my love and passion for walking. Although I would get out and walk three miles with the dog every day, it felt empty, not the same anymore. My passion had gone. I would walk and look around, but nothing had that same feeling, I was numb.

I assume that is the grief, the hurting, the pain. Losing my grandad that I have known for 48 years; it was the hardest thing. Harder than even doing that last walk, which I thought was one of the hardest things to do, especially as I was walking knowing that he may have slipped away as I walked.

But then after a few weeks had passed, and I was busy helping organise his funeral and preparing myself to walk with him on his last moments as a coffin bearer, I saw a friend in our local supermarket who asked me, how I was doing?

After a short conversation about how we were all just getting through like you do, she asked about my walking and I had mentioned that my love had died, but she said, it would come back, just give it time.

She said how she missed seeing my photos and my stories about where I was heading and what I had seen. How she loved sitting in the office and feeling like she had done that walk with me, because I had shown her where I had been and what I had seen.

That night, this played on my mind, that actually, I realised just how many people were watching where I was going and what I was doing and saying the same thing, how much they loved reading and seeing where I was venturing out.

The following day, I could have quite easily just come back in and sat on the sofa, after doing the school run, just going over things in my head. I was so tired all the time, had lost my get up and go. But that day, instead of wallowing I picked up my walking boots and I thought, I am going to get out there.

I knew grandad would not want me to be unhappy and not do the things that I loved. Getting back out there that day has actually helped me. It helped and still is helping me grieve now for both my nan and my grandad.

Walking back in nature enables me to have all of those memories flowing all the time and thinking about both of them. My passion's come back so nature is definitely a healer. I still burst into tears when I walk pass a cricket field remembering those special days that I had with both of them, but that is good as those memories remind me of those good times.

I am so glad that day I conquered my mind and actually put my walking boots back on, because I have my love back. I have realised I needed to be training for my next Ultra Marathon, which is my memorial walk for grandad, and there are lot of hills to conquer.

So, I am getting back to lots of hill training over the South Downs and I may even venture over to the North Downs to see what I am letting myself in for. However, I may keep that as a surprise for the day as for me I find I can walk better and for longer when I do not know where I am heading and that is all part of the new adventure.

I truly do believe for anyone going through such sad, horrible times, if you can get out in nature, it does have a healing power. It gives you space to think. Not only is it good for you and helps with your health, but it helps so much with your mind, and it allows you to process things.

It gives you the headspace that you need without anyone else talking in your ear, phones going off or just the daily noise that surrounds your day. Being out in nature where you are just simply listening to the birds, the wind in the trees, or listening to the rain. It is your time, and it is the space you need. And however, you need healing, nature has a funny way of helping you on your way.

So, my future for me is carrying on, doing what I love, walking in nature, discovering new paths, taking on new challenges and adventures. I will continue with my long weekly challenges and no doubt when I have finished my next Ultra Challenge, I will be looking for the next challenge.

All the time my body allows, I shall be carrying on walking, beating the pain of EDS, arthritis, and Raynaud's, coping with the grief and the loss, and challenging myself further with my walking friend whilst raising money and awareness of charities and worthy causes.

Something I genuinely love about doing these Ultra-Challenges is the support, kindness, and inspiration that you get from other walkers and runners undertaking that same journey. I remember walking on my last challenge, and although I was walking on my own, I never felt alone because there were always people that would chat to you.

Everyone has a story to tell, and people are so open, honest, and understanding. One thing that really helped me on my recent challenge was a lady coming up behind me on my first stop, I did not catch her name and she would say, *"all right, Vicky, how are you getting on?"* I thought to myself, do I know you? How do you know my name?

I then realised that you have your name printed on the back of your number. At that point, I just felt so overwhelmed with appreciation and joy as well as the tears hit me of what was also going on back at home. There are just so many kind and uplifting people that check in on you and make sure you are all right, and they can see when you are struggling and need a lift.

We all are going through our own traumas and problems in life and being kind to others, sharing your experiences, your positive vibes and appreciation goes so far in helping others with their healing.

I hope that by sharing my book and my experiences today I am able to help by encouraging others to get out in nature, walking however far you can, putting one foot in front of the other, and finding positives about every day. Life is too short, and we never know what the future holds for us.

For me, I have turned an incredibly sad event into a positive move forward in creating this book. It has enabled me to start my grieving process, capturing all my childhood memories alongside the events that have happened over the last couple of years, in a book I can share with my children and with others fighting their own battles.

I am now focusing on my next challenge which is the 25km North Downs Challenge in memory of my Grandad and to raise money for Rotherlea Nursing Home in Petworth to thank them for everything they did in caring for my dear Grandad.

Looking back to the past I do not know where I found my inner strength and power from but somehow you can fight and grow and look forward to the future. I am enjoying this journey once again and looking very forward to my next chapters in life.

My Raynaud's Diagnosis and Journey

Looking back now, I realise that I have always suffered with Raynaud's, but all those years ago when I was a teenager, I didn't know what it was. I had always remembered suffering with cold hands and feet and did not think anything of it, I just thought I had cold blood and a warm heart.

It did not matter what the air temperature was I would still be cold. When going on holiday, it could be hot, 34 degrees and my body would still be cold. I would be grabbing those extra duvets out the cupboard and putting extra pairs of socks on my feet because I had ice cold feet, and yet again I just could not warm them. I thought it was simply the way I was built, and I continued accepting that was my body and carrying on with my life.

Then just over 12 years ago, I really started to notice things were becoming harder to deal with. In Winter, I would really struggle with my hands and my feet; chilblains, pain, and lack of movement in my joints, white fingers and just feeling cold right through to the bone.

One particular time when it was at its worst was when I had just started my new business, The Tall Dog, in Midhurst. It was the yearly Christmas Street Party in December, and I had been open late in the evening to show our support to the town and let people know what services I would be offering to local businesses.

As the evening finished and we were slowing down I remember walking down to the local supermarket, my feet and my hands were ice cold, as it had been a very chilly December evening.

Although I had my gloves on and extra socks it just did not seem to make any difference. As I started to walk back, I couldn't put my toes down on the floor as it had become so painful, so it took me over 20 minutes to get back to the shop walking on the sides of my feet (what would normally take 5) and I had tears in my eyes as it really became unbearable.

When I got home, they were red raw, and I thought I would get into the bath and warm them up. However, the pain got worse. It was excruciating as they warmed up, the pain in my feet had reached its worst ever point, and that is the day that became my turning point that I had to see what was going on.

Going to the doctors about what was happening I was diagnosed with Raynaud's and advised to just buy some extra warm merino wool socks and try to just keep warm and not get stressed. Easier said than done as putting on extra socks and extra gloves to try to keep warm did not make any difference. I could have five jumpers on sixteen pairs of socks, and I could not warm up.

It was so deep inside, the pain, like it was right in the middle of my bones and at times it was really, really unbearable.

I carried on trying to deal with this new life of pain and discomfort that could hit you at any time of the year, not just winter and battled through as what other option did, I have. Then one day something happened that finally enabled me to get the treatment that helped me so much through my journey.

Preparing the final stages to opening a new office in the Midhurst High Street, I was just painting the last bit of the signage out in the street, making sure it was perfect for the opening day. I slipped and fell off a ladder when I was high up and fell straight down onto the pavement and broke both of my elbows. Great timing when you are about to open and new premises.

A few months into my recovery which seemed to be taking a much longer time than expected I could not bend my fingers because they were so swollen. After seeing the doctor, she recommended I went to A&E as she thought it was the worst case of Raynaud's she had seen, and I ventured down to A&E on a Friday afternoon to be seen.

Michael met me at the hospital when he had finished work, and they were giving me injections as they thought I had a blood clot developing in my elbow and that could be a reason it was not healing that well.

Then the doctor that they could see I had Raynaud's and thought that I needed to start having special treatment because this is a severe case of Raynaud's. He put me forward for iloprost infusions as he felt this is what was needed.

At that point I was signed up to a rheumatologist and they started me after a while on iloprost infusions, which every winter I would go down to Bognor Hospital for three or four sessions where I would sit for 7 hours at 8 hours at a time, where they'd infuse me with what I called my 'Gold Winter Blood'.

That helped me get through the Winters when the symptoms where at its worst and I did that for several years and was able to cope much better with the condition.

I would still have flare ups and as I learnt more about Raynaud's I started to understand my trigger points. Stress was a major factor, which I did not realise just how much it would affect me.

Whether I was physically stressed or emotionally stressed it triggered more flare ups and something I had to learn to control, but that was hard. I did not know how.

As time went on, I started to develop other symptoms including itching all over. Even now it feels like I have ants crawling all over me all of the time, particularly at night times when I would get into bed and pull a duvet over me. I remember one really incredible rheumatologist, unfortunately, who is retired now, and he explained to me that my nerve endings were on fire as and when my body heated up, that it was like a fibre optic cable that came alive.

That helped me understand the itchiness that I would get all of the time and now have to live with, by taking an antihistamine it takes that slight edge off to help me through the night.

The itching is still a massive symptom for me every day 365 days of the year and can become one of the most irritating parts of the condition.

The other hard part to deal with is the joint pain that it comes with it, and I could always look at my inflammation markers by looking at the little bright brown capillary lines under my fingernails which would give me signal that I was having a flare up. I always remember my specialist saying to keep an eye on that, as that was a good indicator.

One thing that people do assume with Raynaud's is that it is just to do with the cold, but it is not. It is actually to do with the change in temperature. So, it can go from hot to cold, or cold to damp, or damp to hot and it only has to change a few degrees to have influence on my day. It is the change in temperature that causes the problems. It is not just having a freezing day, which I suppose is what people think this is the cause.

I know everyone's condition is different and the level of whiteness in the fingers and the pain that they get is different, but for me, it's the internal deep joint pain that you get and you can't touch it with painkillers, it's so deep inside and I always describe it as I could draw my skeleton to you because I can feel every single bone in my body because it hurts.

Sometimes the only thing that I found warmed me up was having a hot bath and a hot chocolate to warm me up inside. But the heat comes with its own problems too.

When I have a bath, I have to jump in and get my toes out of the water quickly, because otherwise my pain in my toes get to me. Also, there is no point asking me how hot that cup of tea is because I can put my hands around a hot cup of tea and not realise it is hot, it is probably just warm, because my temperature controls are all mixed up.

The temperature control is a is a massive thing for me more so now, which I know with the menopause makes it worse but as I am now understanding the EDS, I understand that there is a real connection between both Raynaud's and EDS.

So, you carry on trying different medications which I am now on which are currently working, and I don't have to go in for my 'Gold Blood' now, but things can always change, flare ups can happen, and it is being more away of your system and your trigger points to help control them.

I was thankful that I broke my elbows because I finally got real treatment to help me. They say things happen for a reason and I genuinely believe that. Since then, I have been more on the radars of rheumatology, and they also have helped me with the recent diagnosis of EDS for which I am also grateful.

My recent increase in walking has definitely helped me with my Raynaud's because when I am out walking, and I am also destressing without necessarily realising it. I honestly believe that this has helped me as my symptoms have been improving, with only the odd real big flare up which is normally connected to an emotional event like my recent flare up when my grandad passed.

So, for me, if I could offer any support and help to others suffering with Raynaud's I think I would suggest venturing out in nature, getting you heart pumping and see if this helps you.

My health now I feel more in control of, and I am sure it is to do with the walking, as in turn it is helping with my mental health and my mindset being able to conquer my pain barriers.

SCLERODERMA & RAYNAUD'S UK

Scleroderma and Raynaud's UK is the only charity dedicated to improving the lives of people affected by Scleroderma and Raynaud's. We exist to improve awareness and understanding of these conditions, to **support those affected**, and ultimately to find a cure.

Call: **020 3893 5998**   Email: info@sruk.co.uk Free Helpline 0800 311 2756
www.sruk.co.uk

My Ehler Danlos Syndrome (EDS) Journey

Days like today, I wake up and everything seems to hurt, my bones, my joints, and my neck in particular. These are the days that you feel like you could just crawl back into bed and just sleep it off, but that doesn't make it go away as it is still there when you wake up, so you just have to get up and deal with it before it takes control of you.

My first diagnosis of being Hypermobile with EDS actually came before I had my operation in February 22, which was lucky as I could provide that to the surgeons before I went under the knife! Thank God that I had the conversation with the specialist regards to my Rectocele that I had been diagnosed with by the doctor back in July 21 as where I am today may have been so different.

It came about as during that conversation when I was explaining what I had experienced as a child, things that I didn't even think were relevant, like having hip dysplasia, bruising by simply touching the table, being able to do the splits and sitting cross legged with my knees right down, twisting around like an owl and my skin being extra stretchy.

I did not realise that was not a normal thing to do, I thought everyone was like this. But for me this was my normal, this was me, yet I was not prepared that it would come to haunt me as an adult.

As I continued discussing about the various things that had happened when I was a child, like dislocating my kneecap when I was in primary school, twisting my vertebrates in my back in secondary school, and when I broke my elbows, when I fell off a ladder just over 12 years ago, all of them taking so long to heal, longer than normal he suspected this could be down to suffering with EDS, which makes such sense to me now.

The more I am learning about EDS, the more I realise that there are now reasons why my body is doing what it does and why it takes longer to heal. It is why I have to now work on myself to keep my body stronger inside, especially as everything tends to move about with that extra elasticity you have with EDS, and yet another reason to explain my early onset of prolapses!

So, one of the best things that came out of that day was this diagnosis of EDS that can often take 10 years to diagnose.

In May 24 after seeing my rheumatologist about a flare up with my Raynaud's I was experiencing, which I now realise was to do with the huge emotional stress, he explained that the EDS was also a huge factor. The yoga I had been doing is great, but I had to watch that I did not overdo it, especially with my neck as I did not want to aggravate this anymore.

Having an exceptionally good yoga teacher that understands my condition and would tell me when I was bending too far enabled me to continue what I loved.

It becomes frustrating as often I am not aware just how far I am twisting or bending as it is natural for me. You also find that you have to bend further or twist further to feel like you are actually doing something, but then you also have to be careful as you can actually damage yourself by things popping out like my hip bone used to do (and also my jaw has started to if I spend the day talking!) and that is where my teacher helps me.

Currently my EDS journey has given me a new problem with my neck which is causing an awful lot of pain, and mobility and weakness issues with my hands and arms.

Seeing the impacts on my wrists and my shoulders already is worrying. My ability to not grip things for long periods, problems with unscrewing lids, lifting the kettle when it's full, carrying bags of shopping, filling a flask from the kettle, all things that I used to be able to do automatically, now I have to accept some days I just simply can't do it anymore.

I have good days and bad days. Some days there is nothing wrong and other days everything is a mission, but I have now learnt over time to accept this is just the way it is. This is part of both my EDS and my Raynaud's and sometimes it is difficult to know which ones is which as there is such a crossover between the two. My journey now is to learn more about how it affects me and how I can overcome the problems I have. I am not giving into this, and walking is really helping me fight both of these.

Even though there are days where I feel that I have aged 30 years overnight and my body is just living in the body of an older person, I carry on. With the walking, it enables me to try and forget what is going on with my body. Yes, it is challenging, and at times when you start out walking, you're in an awful lot of pain, however within 10-20 minutes of walking and constantly looking around in nature and observing what is happening with the trees, the birds, the air and the smells I am able to forget and take my mind off of my pain. This is how walking has really helped with my EDS & Raynaud's.

If you suffer with EDS, then why not visit the website, and see how they can help you too but also try walking. Walking has helped so much. Walking is helping me deal with my EDS and Raynaud's. Walking has given me a new mindset. It is enabling me to be in control of my life again.

When the pain gets too much, I just learn to accept it. I have good days and I have bad days and on those good days, I choose to thrive and get out there and do what I can. On the bad days, I just let my body recover and heal. I cannot change my diagnosis, but I can change my mind and how I deal with my days.

The Ehlers-Danlos Society:
www.ehlers-danlos.org

Discovery of The Ultra Challenge Series

My New Passion

The Ultra Challenge have been such an amazing part of my journey and have given me such new confidence and self-belief in myself to achieve what I have today. I really believe that if I had not ventured out that day 1 year after my operation, taking on new adventures in walking, looking for a challenging event that I could test myself and raise money and awareness for a charity close to my heart, I would not be doing what I am today.

My life really has changed because of them, and I am so proud of myself for what I have achieved. I am truly looking forward to all the new challenges that I can take on all the time I am physically able to. I plan to work my way through the events, keep repeating them, challenging myself further, making new friends on the way and being part of a walking family. This is what it feels like I have gained, and I hope one day you can experience this for yourself.

Whether you are new to walking, or an experienced walker, they have events for everyone. You can work your way up to larger ones, stick at small ones, it really does not matter, taking that step to crossing that start line in itself is such an achievement.

We are all different, we have varied reasons for doing what we do, we all have a story, and this is just mine and I hope you have enjoyed reading it.

Stay Strong, plan your adventure, get out into Nature, and enjoy everything that it offers you.

Remember it is not how long you have walked, how many miles you have conquered, it is breaking that habit and changing your way of thinking. Start off saying I can do this, I can get out there for 5 minutes, then 10, then 20.

Don't Give Up – You are Stronger than you think.

References and Links

SCLERODERMA & RAYNAUD'S UK

Scleroderma and Raynaud's UK is the only charity dedicated to improving the lives of people affected by Scleroderma and Raynaud's. We exist to improve awareness and understanding of these conditions, to support those affected, and ultimately to find a cure.

Call: 020 3893 5998   Email: info@sruk.co.uk
Free Helpline 0800 311 2756

www.sruk.co.uk

The Ehlers-Danlos Society:

www.ehlers-danlos.org

Dementia UK is the specialist dementia nursing charity that is there for the whole family. Its nurses, known as Admiral Nurses, provide life-changing support with all forms of dementia.
 Find information and advice Visit dementiauk.org/information-and-support for information on all aspects of dementia.
 Contact Dementia UK's free Helpline
Call 0800 888 6678 (Monday-Friday 9am-9pm, Saturday and Sunday 9am-5pm, every day except 25th December) or
email **helpline@dementiauk.org**
 Book a virtual clinic appointment
Book a phone or video appointment with an Admiral Nurse at dementiauk.org/book

The Macmillan Cancer Support

Line offers confidential support to people living with cancer and their loved ones. If you need to talk, we listen.

Telephone: 0808 808 00 00

www.macmillan.org.uk

Prostate Cancer Research
info@pcr.org.uk
0203 7355444
23 – 24 Great James Street
London WC1N 3ES

www.prostate-cancer-research.org.uk

Ultra Challenge Series
Telephone 0207 609 6695
Email: **info@ultrachallenge.com**

www.ultrachallenge.com

AllTrails: Trail Guides & Maps for Hiking, Camping, and Running | AllTrails
www.alltrails.com

Acknowledgements

Where do I start as there are so many people to thank that have been and continue to be amazing throughout my journey.

Firstly, my partner Michael, who has stood by me with continued support and strength, giving up his time when I was recovering, making sure I had everything I could possibly need, and for getting me through my most painful and unbearable times, for being my taxi driver for all my checkups and appointments and being there by my side through my darkest hours.

My Mum and Dad, who took looked after Harry whilst I was recovering, and you were recovering too.

To my dear friend Jess, who was my complete rock, that I could contact any time of day, when I was in tears, when I was frustrated and when I simply didn't know where to turn next.

My dear friends Amber and Emma, who throughout both their battles with Cancer themselves, still continued providing support, energy and encouragement even through battling their hardest times of their lives.

To the surgeons, specialists and physios who helped me through every stage of my diagnosis, surgery and recovery.

Not forgetting my walking friend Samo who will continue with me on my new adventures, .and to my walking friends who trusted me on my new adventures whilst training for my events. Apologies for all those muddy routes we conquered.

To my dear nan and grandad, who showed me what true love really meant. My grandad for looking after nan the way you did, on your own through Covid and her dementia, and for the team at Rotherlea that gave grandad the ultimate care during his time with you and in his last days where you showed me the love and care that you truly had for him.

To all the other individuals and families going through surgery, a Dementia Journey, Battling Cancer, EDS, Raynaud's or any other syndrome or disease and those who suffer everyday with Chronic Pain and continue to push themselves to their limits.

Also, to myself for not giving up, for fighting, becoming stronger, breaking those pain barriers and overcoming those challenges, letting others help, slowing down and pushing myself into things that I never thought was possible.

This book has been for you all, and I thank you for reading it and letting me share my journey with you xx

About the Author

Vicki Harrison is happiest when she is venturing out in the countryside with Samo, her four-legged walking buddy.

With her newfound 'Walking Addiction', since surgery left her relearning how to walk, you may see her wandering around the South Downs with a takeaway coffee in one hand and the dog lead and phone, dealing with emails as she walks in the other.

A proud mum of two boys Jack and Harry, and a Small Business Owner of The Tall Dog, she lives in Midhurst with her partner, teenage son and Samo.

When she is not out walking, she will be working on her client accounts, designing websites or off cycling in nature. Other days, you may find out lunching with her partner in crime supporting local businesses as they support her.

And if she is not doing that, then she will be planning and training for her next Ultra Challenge or Walking Adventure with her favourite walking App.

As your works out the next way to raise money for charity, she will be booking upon her next event whether it be walking an Ultra Marathon, jumping out of a plane or abseiling the Spinnaker Tower or Arundel Castle.

No one every knows what she is planning next, but she is living her life to the full. She reminds us that we only get one shot at life and therefore you have to enjoy it.

I invite you now to visit my website and discover my walks in colour where you can see many of my photographs that I took on my adventures.

Enjoy www.coatoncoatoffwetfeet.uk

Printed in Great Britain
by Amazon